The O'Neal's Way
"BIG BACK" Edition
Recipe Book

INTRODUCTION

Welcome to

"The O'Neal's Way: 'Big Back' Edition,"

A culinary journey inspired by the hearty, flavorful, and soul-nourishing recipes cherished by the O'Neal family for generations. This collection celebrates the rich traditions of home-cooked meals, bringing together a variety of dishes that embody comfort, warmth, and the joy of sharing food with loved ones.

In this special edition, we focus on the "Big Back" philosophy – an ode to robust flavors, generous portions, and the art of creating meals that satisfy both the body and the soul. From succulent roasts and savory stews to decadent desserts and everything in between, each recipe has been crafted with love, care, and a touch of The O'Neal family magic.

Whether you're a seasoned cook or a kitchen novice, this book is designed to guide you through each step with ease and confidence. We aim to inspire you to create memorable meals, infusing your creativity while staying true to the essence of The O'Neal's Way.

Join us as we explore a world where food is more than just sustenance—it's a way to connect, celebrate, and savor the moments that matter most. Let's get cooking and make every meal a masterpiece!

Feel free to adjust or add any personal touches that reflect your unique style and the essence of your family's culinary traditions.

Table of Contents

APPETIZERS

HONEY BUFFALO WINGS

INGREDIENTS:

- (2) lb. Fresh Cut Chicken Wings
- Fresh Rosemary
- Fresh Parsley
- 3 tbsp. Lemon Juice
- 4 tbsp. Butter
- 6 tbsp. French's Stone Ground Dijon Mustard
- 1/2 cup Honey
- 1 cup Franks RedHot Sauce
- 4 cups Cooking Oil

SEASONINGS:

- 2 tsp. Spice Theory Garlic Herb Pepper Blend
- 2 tbsp. Chicken Seasoning
- 2 tbsp. Cajun Seasoning

DIRECTIONS:

1. Remove the wings from the package, rinse them in cool water and lemon juice, and pat them dry. Next, place the wings in a bowl and add French's Stone Ground Dijon Mustard, freshly chopped Parsley, Chicken seasoning, and Cajun seasoning.
2. Massage the ingredients into the wings thoroughly, ensuring the wings are evenly coated.
3. Preheat your choice of cooking oil to 350-365 degrees. While the oil is heating up, add a few rosemary sprigs to boost the flavor as we fry the wings.
4. Once the oil is ready, begin adding the wings. Depending on how many you have to cook, add only 5-7 at a time to ensure they all cook evenly.
5. Fry the wings for 12-15 minutes or until they reach an internal temperature of 165 degrees. After cooking, remove them from the oil and place them on a wire rack to drain any extra oil.
6. Place the wings into a bowl and set them aside to prepare the Honey Buffalo Sauce.

Honey Buffalo Sauce

1. In a medium saucepan on medium/low heat, add Butter, Franks RedHot Buffalo Sauce, Honey, Lemon Juice, and Spice Theory Garlic Herb Pepper Blend, mixing well.
2. Allow the sauce to simmer. After it has simmered for a few minutes, grab the bowl of chicken and pour the sauce over the wings.
3. Place a cover over the wings, then shake and toss, making sure every piece is covered in that delicious sauce!
4. Plate your wings and serve them with your favorite sides, along with Ranch! Enjoy!

HONEY LEMON PEPPER RANCH WINGS

 4 Servings   *Recipe*   *30 Minutes*

INGREDIENTS:

- 2 lbs Whole Wings
- Fresh Rosemary Spriggs
- Freshly Squeezed Lemon Juice
- Fresh Lemon Zest
- Fresh Parsley
- 3 cups Peanut Cooking
- Oil 2 cups Lefty's Spices
- Chicken Flour Mix
- 4 tbsp Honey
- 4 tbsp Mustard
- 6 tbsp Butter, SALTED

SEASONINGS:

- 2/3 cup Hidden Valley Ranch Seasoning
- 2 tsp Simply Spice Garlic Herb Lemon Pepper Seasoning
- 2 tsp Simply Spice All-Purpose Seasoning
- 2 tsp Smoked Paprika
- 2 tsp Black Pepper

DIRECTIONS:

1. Remove wings from the package and cut them down into separate pieces. Then place them in a large mixing bowl. Clean the chicken with Vinegar and limes then pat them dry and move to the next step.
2. Next, add Mustard as your binder, followed by your seasonings, Garlic Herb Lemon Pepper Seasoning, All-Purpose Seasoning and Smoked Paprika then mix.
3. To a medium mixing bowl combine Lefty's Spices Chicken Flour Mix and a forth cup of Hidden Valley Ranch Seasoning then mix until well combined.
4. Next, add the wings to the flour mixture then give them a good toss and shake until they are fully coated.
5. In a large boiling pot, pour in Peanut Cooking Oil on medium/high heat and a few Fresh Rosemary Spriggs. Once the oil has reached a temperature of 350 degrees, begin adding in the Wings.
6. Allow the wings to cook for 7-9 minutes while stirring occasionally or until the chicken reaches an internal temp of 165 degrees.

7. Once the wings have finished cooking, remove them from the oil and place them on a wire rack to drain off the extra grease. Set them aside to prepare Honey Lemon Pepper Sauce.

Honey Buffalo Sauce

1. In a medium saucepan on low heat, melt some Salted Butter. Once melted, pour in some Honey, along with fresh Lemon Zest, freshly squeezed Lemon Juice., fresh Parsley and Black Pepper then mix.
2. Bring your sauce to a simmer by raising the temp a bit. Once the sauce has simmered for 1-2 minutes, turn off the heat and get ready to pour over the wings.
3. Add your Wings to a mixing bowl then pour the Honey Lemon Pepper Sauce all over them. Sprinkle on a couple teaspoons more of the Hidden Valley Rach seasoning then give them a good toss! Plate and garnish with some parsley with some ranch dressing on the side and ENJOY!

HONEY JERK WINGS

 1-4 Servings   *Recipe*   *40 Minutes*

INGREDIENTS:
- (8) Whole Chicken Wings
- 1 tbsp. Walkerswood MildJerk Seasoning
- 1 tbsp. Honey
- 2 tbsp Water
- 2 tbsp Fresh Lemon Juice
- 3 tbsp. Minced Garlic
- 3 tbsp. Minced Ginger
- 1/2 cup. Low-Sodium Soy Sauce
- 1/2 cup. Olive Oil

SEASONINGS:
- 2 tbsp. Chicken Seasoning
- 2 tbsp. Spice Theory Jerk Spice Rub

DIRECTIONS:
1. Preheat the oven to 375 degrees.
2. Remove the Wings from the package, pat dry, and drizzle on some olive oil then season with Chicken seasoning and Spice Theory Jerk Spice Rub. Be sure to massage the seasonings into the Wings thoroughly.
3. In a 12-inch skillet on medium/high heat, drizzle two tablespoons of Olive Oil over the wings. Sear the Wings for 3-5 minutes on each side to get a nice char, then remove them from the skillet and onto a large baking dish.
4. Place the baking dish into the 375-degree oven for 35 minutes. Once the time has passed, remove the wings from the oven and set aside to prepare the Honey Jerk sauce.
5. In a small saucepan on medium/low heat, pour in another two tablespoons of Olive Oil along with minced garlic and ginger. Saute the garlic and ginger for a couple of minutes, then reduce the heat to low.
6. Next, pour in some low-sodium Soy Sauce, Walkerswood Mild Jerk seasoning, Honey, and a little water for balance.

7. Allow the sauce to come to a simmer, then add the wings to the skillet and baste them in the sauce. Turn off the heat, and you're all done!
8. Pair these wings with your favorite sides and ENJOY!

OVEN-ROASTED BBQ JERK WINGS

 4 Servings   Recipe   50 Minutes

INGREDIENTS:
- (8) Jumbo Whole Wings
- 2 tbsp Grace Jamaican Jerk Seasoning
- 3 tbsp Worcestershire Sauce
- 3 tbsp Mike's Hot Honey
- 3 tbsp White Distilled Vinegar
- 4 tbsp Butter, SALTED
- 1 cup Ketchup
- 1/2 cup Mustard
- 1/4 cup Pineapple Mango Juice
- 1/4 cup Zesty Italian Dressing
- 2/3 cups Brown Sugar

SEASONINGS:
- 2 tsp Spiceology Mother Plucker Poultry Rub
- 2 tsp Cajun Seasoning
- 2 tsp Spice King Country BBQ Rub
- 4 tsp PS Seasoning Texas BBQ Rodeo Rub
- 2 tsp Chili Powder
- 2 tsp White Pepper
- 2 tsp Roasted Ground Cumin

DIRECTIONS:
1. Preheat the oven to 400 degrees
2. Remove wings from the package and cut them down into separate pieces. Then, place them in a large mixing bowl. Clean the chicken with Vinegar and lemons, then pat them dry and move to the next step.
3. Next, season them with Spiceology Mother Plucker Poultry Rub, Cajun Seasoning, and Spice King Country BBQ Rub, then pour some Zesty Italian Dressing and a couple of teaspoons of Grace Jamaican Jerk Seasoning and mix.
4. Lay the wings on a wire rack, then place them into the oven to cook for 45 minutes, making sure you flip the wings halfway through the cooking process.
5. Once complete, remove them from the oven, place them in a medium mixing bowl, and set them aside to create the Homemade BBQ Sauce.
6. Melt half a stick of Butter in a small skillet on medium/low heat, and once the butter has melted, add in Ketchup, Mustard, Worcestershire Sauce,

White Vinegar, Mikes Hot Honey, Pineapple Juice, Brown Sugar, White Pepper, Chili Powder, Cumin, PS Seasoning Texas BBQ Rodeo Rub then mix until well combined.

7. Allow the sauce to come to a simmer, and once it does, turn off the heat and pour half of the sauce onto the wing inside the mixing bowl. Give them a toss, place the wings back onto the wire rack, and put them back in the oven for 5-7 minutes. Just long enough to seal in the flavors from the Homemade BBQ Sauce!

8. Once the time goes off in the oven, it is time to add these wings to a couple of plates with a side of ranch dressing and ENJOY!

PEPSI STICKY WINGS

INGREDIENTS:
- (8) Whole Chicken Wings
- (1) 7 oz. can Pepsi
- 1 tsp. Cornstarch
- 2 tbsp Water
- 3 tbsp. Minced Garlic
- 3 tbsp. Minced Ginger
- /2 cup. Olive Oil
- 1/4 cup. Low-Sodium Soy Sauce
- 1/4 cup. Water

SEASONINGS:
- 2 tbsp. Cajun Seasoning
- 2 tbsp. Nicks Of Clinton Branded Pepper Seasoning
- 2 tbsp. Smoked Paprika

DIRECTIONS:
1. Preheat the oven to 375 degrees.
2. Remove the Wings from the package, pat dry, and drizzle on some olive oil then season with Cajun Seasoning, Nicks Of Clinton Branded Pepper Seasoning, and Smoked Paprika. Be sure to massage the seasonings into the Wings thoroughly.
3. In a 12-inch skillet on medium/high heat, drizzle two tablespoons of Olive Oil over the wings. Sear the Wings for 3-5 minutes on each side to get a nice char, then remove them from the skillet and onto a large baking dish.
4. Place the baking dish into the 375-degree oven for 35 minutes. Once the time has passed, remove the wings from the oven and set aside to prepare the Sticky Pepsi sauce.
5. In the same skillet the wings was prepared in on medium/low heat, pour in another two tablespoons of Olive Oil along with minced garlic and ginger. Saute the garlic and ginger for a couple of minutes, then reduce the heat to low.

6. Next, pour in the full can of Pepsi along with some low-sodium Soy Sauce, and a Cornstarch Slurry made with a little water and cornstarch mixed together.
7. Allow the sauce to come to a simmer and thicken up a bit, then add the wings to the skillet and baste them in the sauce while giving them a little toss for a few minutes to help the sauce stick to the wings. Turn off the heat, and you're all done!
8. Pair these wings with your favorite sides and ENJOY!

BUFFALO CHICKEN EGG ROLLS

 4 Servings   Recipe   20 Minutes

INGREDIENTS:
- (1) Rotisserie Chicken
- (8) Egg Roll Wrappers
- 1/2 White Onion, Diced
- (4) Celery Stalks, Diced
- 3 cups Cooking Oil
- 2 tbsp Garlic & Herb Butter
- 2 tbsp Worcestershire Sauce
- 1 tbsp Stir-in Roasted Garlic Paste
- 1/2 cup Franks Red Hot Buffalo Sauce
- 1/2 Block Philadelphia Cream Cheese, Softened
- (1) Block Colby Jack Cheese, Shredded

SEASONINGS:
- 2 tbsp Badia Complete Seasoning

DIRECTIONS:
1. Begin by breaking down the Rotisserie Chicken into pieces, making it easier to shred the chicken. After slicing the chicken, add it to a mixing bowl and set it aside to prepare the buffalo cheese sauce.
2. In a skillet on medium heat, melt a couple of tablespoons of butter. Once the butter has melted, add diced Onions, Celery, and a little Roasted Garlic paste.
3. Saute veggies for 2 minutes, then season with Badia Complete Seasoning, pour in Worcestershire sauce, Franks Red Hot Buffalo Sauce, and softened Cream Cheese.
4. Give everything a nice mix, then cut off the heat and keep stirring until everything is well combined or until the Cream Cheese melts fully into the sauce.
5. Pour sauce into the same bowl the shredded chicken is in along with some freshly shredded Colby Jack Cheese, then mix until well combined, and now you have a delicious Buffalo Chicken Dip.

6. Combine a little water and cornstarch together; this will be how you seal off the Egg Rolls after rolling them. Grab one egg roll at a time and apply your cornstarch slurry to the edges of the egg rolls.
7. Once you have slurry on the edges, add about a tablespoon of dip to the edge of the egg roll that is closest to you. Please give it a roll, bring the other two edges in, roll once more, and seal off the final edge with more slurry, then repeat with the other egg rolls.
8. In a large boiling pot, add your choice of cooking oil and bring it to a temperature of 350 degrees. Once oil is ready, add Egg Rolls a few at a time. Fry them for 5-7 minutes or until golden brown.
9. When they are done, remove them from the grease and place them on a wire rack to drain any extra oil, and you are all done! Now to make the Spicy ranch sauce!

SPICY RANCH SAUCE
1. In a mixing bowl, add the Ranch Dressing of your choosing, Franks Red Hot Buffalo Sauce, and Badia Garlic and Herb Seasoning, then mix!
2. Pour this sauce over your Egg Rolls or have it as a dipping sauce. Either way, ENJOY!

CHICKEN FAJITA EGG ROLLS

 4 Servings Recipe 35 Minutes

INGREDIENTS:

- (10) Egg Roll Wrappers
- (6) Boneless Chicken Thighs
- (1) White Onion, Sliced
- (1) Yellow Bell Pepper, Sliced
- (1) Red Bell Pepper, Sliced
- 2 tbsp Stir-in Chunky Garlic Paste
- 3 tbsp Butter, Salted
- 3 tbsp Parsley, Chopped
- 4 tbsp Fresh Lime Juice
- 4 tbsp Fresh Lemon Juice
- 4 tbsp Olive Oil
- 6 tbsp Garlic & Herb Butter
- 2 cups Mozzarella Cheese, Shredded
- 3 cups Cooking Oil

SEASONINGS:

- 3 tsp Kinders Italian Chop House Seasoning
- 3 tsp Badia Sazon Tropical Seasoning
- 3 tsp Cajun Seasoning
- 3 tsp Garlic & Herb Seasoning

DIRECTIONS:

1. Begin by removing the chicken thighs from the package, drying off the moisture, and placing them in a mixing bowl.
2. Next, drizzle in two tablespoons of Olive Oil, then season with Kinder's Italian Chop House Seasoning, Badia Sazon Tropical Seasoning, Cajun Seasoning, a tablespoon of chopped Parsley, and two tablespoons of fresh Lime Juice. Mix.
3. In a 12-inch skillet on medium/high heat, pour in a couple tablespoons of Olive Oil, followed by the chicken thighs. Cook the chicken thighs on each side for 6-8 minutes.
4. Once the thighs have finished cooking, turn off the heat and remove them from the skillet to a cutting board. Dice the thighs into 2-inch cubes, then place them in a bowl and set aside.

5. In the same skillet the chicken was prepared in, crank the heat to medium and melt some salted Butter. Once melted, add some Garlic Paste, then begin adding the vegetables: sliced White Onions, Yellow Bell Peppers, and Red Bell Peppers.
6. Saute the veggies for 6-8 minutes just before the onions become translucent, then add the diced chicken thighs back to the skillet, give everything a good mix, and cut the heat.
7. Combine a little water and cornstarch in a bowl; this will be the mixture to seal off the Egg Rolls after rolling them. Grab one egg roll at a time and apply your cornstarch slurry to the edges of the egg rolls.
8. Once you have slurry on the edges, add shredded Mozzarella Cheese, your Chicken Fajita mix, and more Mozzarella Cheese to the edge of the egg roll that is closest to you.
9. Give it a roll, bring the other two edges in, roll once more, and seal off the final edge with more slurry, then repeat with the other egg rolls.
10. Add your cooking oil to a large boiling pot and bring it to 350 degrees. Once the oil is ready, add Egg Rolls a few at a time. Fry them for 5-7 minutes or until golden brown.
11. When done, remove them from the grease and place them on a wire rack to drain any extra oil. Then you are all done! Enjoy a few with a cilantro lime ranch on the side and ENJOY!

SPINACH CRAB DIP EGG ROLLS

 4 Servings   *Recipe*   *20 Minutes*

INGREDIENTS:
- (10) Egg Roll Wrappers
- 16 oz Jumbo Lump Crab Meat
- 1 tbsp Stir-in Chunky Garlic Paste
- 4 tbsp Fresh Lemon Juice
- 6 tbsp Garlic & Herb Butter
- 6 tbsp Crystals Hot Sauce
- 1/2 Block Philadelphia Cream Cheese, Softened
- (1) Block Mozzarella Cheese, Shredded
- (1) Block Sharp Cheddar Cheese, Shredded
- 1/4 cup Mustard
- 2/3 cup Ketchup
- 1/2 cup Mayo
- 3 cups Cooking Oil
- 4 cups Baby Spinach

SEASONINGS:
- 3 tbsp Badia Complete Seasoning
- 3 tbsp Spice King Gourmet Seafood seasoning
- 3 tbsp Very Good Garlic by Tabitha Brown
- 2 tbsp Smoked Paprika
- 1 tbs Garlic & Herb seasoning
- 1 tbs All-Purpose

DIRECTIONS:
1. Begin by adding Avocado Oil to a skillet on medium heat, along with some chunky garlic paste. Next, add the spinach and Badia Complete Seasoning, and cook it for 4-6 minutes.
2. Once done, remove the spinach from the heat, then add the spinach to a mixing bowl along with the Jumbo Lump Crab meat.
3. Next, pour in some melted Kerry Gold Garlic and herb butter, shredded Mozzarella and Cheddar Cheese, half a block of Philadelphia Cream Cheese, Grey Poupon Mustard, and 3 tbsp of the hot sauce of your choosing.
4. Season the mix with Spice King Gourmet Seafood seasoning, Very Good Garlic seasoning by Tabitha Brown, and Smoked Paprika, then give all the ingredients a good mix, then get ready to roll the crab mixture into the egg rolls.

5. Combine a little water and cornstarch; this will be how you seal off the Egg Rolls after rolling them. Grab one egg roll at a time and apply your cornstarch slurry to the edges of the egg rolls.
6. Once you have slurry on the edges, add about a couple tablespoons of dip to the edge of the egg roll that is closest to you. Give it a roll, bring the other two edges in, roll once more, and seal off the final edge with more slurry, then repeat with the other egg rolls.
7. In a large boiling pot, add your choice of cooking oil and bring it to 350 degrees. Once oil is ready, add Egg Rolls a few at a time. Fry them for 5-7 minutes or until golden brown.
8. When they are done, remove them from the grease and place them on a wire rack to drain any extra oil, and you are all done! Now to make the Homemade Remoulade Sauce!

HOMEMADE REMOULADE SAUCE

1. In a mixing bowl, add the Mayo of your choosing, Ketchup, Mustard, 3 tbsp of Hot Sauce, Garlic and herb seasoning, All-Purpose seasoning, Fresh Parsley, and Lemon Juice, then mix!
2. Add the sauce to a squeeze bottle, pour it over your Egg Rolls, or have it on the side as a dipping sauce. Either way, ENJOY!

BUTTERY CRAB TOAST POINTS

 6 Servings   Recipe   45 Minutes

INGREDIENTS:

- 16oz Jumbo Lump Crab Meat Beget, Foot Long
- 5 Garlic Cloves, Diced
- 1/2 White Onion, Diced Fresh Parsley, Chopped
- 6 tbsp Butter
- 1 tbsp Sherry Cooking Wine
- 1 tbsp Worcestershire Sauce
- 1 tbsp Crystal Hot Sauce
- 1 tbsp Roasted Garlic Paste
- 2 tbsp Garlic & Herb Butter
- 1 tsp Better Than Bouillon Lobster Base
- 2 tsp AP Flour
- 1 cup Half & Half
- 1 cup Heavy Cream
- 1/2 cup Parmesan Cheese, Grated
- 1/4 cup Olive Oil

SEASONINGS:

- 2 tbsp Old Bay Seasoning
- 2 tbsp Delallo's Roasted Garlic & Cheese Seasoning
- 1 tbsp Crushed Red Pepper Flakes
- 1 tbsp White Powder
- 1 tbsp Smoked Paprika

DIRECTIONS:

1. Preheat oven to 350 degrees.
2. Remove Beget from the package, then slice an inch and a half pieces. Once cut, lay them on a wire rack.
3. In a small mixing bowl, pour in Olive Oil, Delallo's Roasted Garlic & Cheese Seasoning, Crushed Red Pepper Flakes, and grated Parmesan Cheese, then mix until well combined.
4. Add the oil you prepared to the tops of the Beget slices by brushing it on evenly on each piece, then top it off with a little more grated Parmesan Cheese.
5. Place rack into the preheated oven and cook them for 5-7 minutes or until you have a nice golden brown on top. Remove them from the oven and set aside to prepare buttery crab topping.
6. In a medium skillet on medium heat, melt a couple of tablespoons of butter and add in Roasted Garlic Paste with 8oz of Jumbo Lump Crab meat.

7. Season the crab meat with your favorite Seafood Seasoning, then mix everything. Cook your crab meat for 2-3 minutes, then remove from heat. (Try not to break down the crab too much because you still want some nice chunks on each toast point.)
8. Now combine your Buttery Crab Meat with the tops of the Toast Points you prepared earlier. Top them off with grated Parmesan Cheese, Parsley Flakes, melted Garlic Butter, and ENJOY!
9. Take your experience to the next level with a Homemade Cream of Crab Soup as a dipping sauce! RECIPE BELOW!

Homemade Cream of Crab Soup
1. In a medium Dutch pot on medium/low heat, add Butter, diced Garlic Cloves, and White Onion. Cook your veggies for 5-7 minutes, add Better Than Bouillon Lobster Base, and stir again.
2. Once those ingredients are well combined, add AP Flour, Half & Half, and Heavy Cream. Allow your soup to come to a slow simmer.
3. Next, add Sherry Cooking Wine, Worcestershire Sauce, Old Bay Seasoning, White Pepper, Smoked Paprika, and Hot Sauce. Mix ingredients well.
4. Allow your soup to simmer for another 5-7 minutes before adding about 8oz of Crab meat and Fresh Parsley to your Crab Soup. (You want to leave a little left as a topping for your soup in the bowl.)
5. Bring the heat to Low and let your soup simmer for 10-15 minutes. Once complete, remove from heat.
6. Grab a bowl and spoon in Cream of Crab Soup alongside your Crab Toast Points and ENJOY!

POT ROAST CORNBREAD SLIDERS

 6 Servings   Recipe   2 Hours 30 Minutes

INGREDIENTS:

- 3 lb Chuck Pot Roast
  2 Eggs
- 3 Yellow Potatoes, Sliced
- 1/2 White Onion, Diced
- 3 Carrots, Sliced
- 3 cups Beef Broth
- 1 tsp Better Than Bouillon Roasted Beef Base
- 1 tbsp Roasted Garlic Paste
- 1 tbsp Baking Powder
- 2 tbsp Tomato Paste
- 1.5 tbsp of AP Flour
- 6 tbsp Avocado Oil
- 4 tbsp Butter
- 1/4 cup Honey
- 1 cup Cornmeal
- 1 cup White Sugar
- 1 cup Whole Milk

SEASONINGS:

- 3 tbsp Kinders Prime Steak Seasoning
- 3 tbsp Delallo's Rosemary Garlic Seasoning
- 1 tsp OSMO White Flaky Salt

DIRECTIONS:

1. Preheat oven to 400 degrees.
2. Remove Chuck Roast from its package, pat dry, then pour in 3 tbsp of Avocado Oil over the Roast, then season the Roast with Kinders Prime Steak Seasoning and Delallo's RosemaryGarlic Seasoning then massage seasonings in thoroughly.
3. In a cast iron dutch oven on medium/high heat add in 3 tbsp of Avocado Oil. Once ready, add the Chuck Roast to the pot and sear on each side for 4-6 minutes on each side.
4. Once finished, remove Chuck Roast and set aside. In the same pot, reduce the heat to medium/low and melt 3 tbsp of Butter. Once melted add in diced Onions, Roasted Garlic Paste, Better Than Bouillon Roasted Beef Base, Tomato Paste, AP Flour, and Beef Broth then mix.
5. Turn off the heat and return the Chuck Roast to the pot, then baste Roast with the juices from the pot, COVER and place pot in the preheated oven for a total of 2 hours.

6. After an hour has passed, flip the Roast, baste the roast, then add in sliced yellow potatoes and carrots, COVER again then place back in the oven for an additional hour.
7. Once time is up, remove pot from oven remove the cover and admire that beautiful roast! Set the Roast aside to prepare Homemade Cornbread.
8. In a large bowl, combine the following, Cornmeal, 1 cup of AP Flour, Baking Powder, White Sugar, OSMO White Flakey Salt, 2 Eggs, Honey, and finally Whole Milk then mix until well combined.
9. Grab a Jumbo Muffin pan and add a little Avocado Oil to a napkin and be sure apply enough oil to the pan to help with muffins not sticking after the cooking process.
10. Pour Cornbread mix into each muffin pan then place in the oven for 15-20 minutes or until golden brown.
11. Once complete, remove them. from oven, cut them in half, and assemble your sliders! Shred your Roast and place on the bottom bun of cornbread, then slice potatoes, then Carrots and finally the gravy from the roast, and top it off with the top of the muffin! Drizzle a little extra honey on top of the muffins and ENJOY!

SPICY BBQ MEATBALL SLIDERS

 3 Servings   *Recipe*   *30 Minutes*

INGREDIENTS:

- 1lb Ground Beef
- 1lb Ground Sausage
- 2 Eggs
- 12 pack Hawaiian Rolls
- 1 Stick Butter, Salted
- 1 cup Barilla Marinara Sauce
- 1 cup Mozzarella Cheese, Shredded
- 1 cup Parmesan Cheese, Shredded
- 1/2 cup Garlic Butter Ritz Crackers, Crushed
- 3 tbsp Worcestershire Sauce
- 3 tbsp Minced Garlic
- 4 tbsp Avocado Oil
- 6 tbsp Parsley, Freshly Chopped

SEASONINGS:

- 3 tbsp Delallo's Garlic & Tomato Seasoning
- 3 tbsp Delallo's Sun-Dried Tomato & Basil Seasoning
- 2 tbsp Delallo's Roasted Garlic & Cheese Seasoning.

DIRECTIONS:

1. Preheat oven to 350 degrees.
2. In a large mixing bowl, combine Ground Beef and Ground Sausage along with 2 Eggs, Garlic Butter Seasoning, All-Purpose Seasoning, PS Smoky BBQ Rodeo Rub, crushed Garlic Butter Ritz Crackers, Parmesan Cheese, and freshly chopped Parsley then mix.
3. Take a tablespoon of your meat mixture into your hand and roll until you make a golf ball size Meatball then place them on a baking dish. Do this repeatedly until you fill the baking dish and if there are any left over, ziplock them and place in freezer for later use.
4. In a 12-inch skillet on medium/high heat, pour in some Avocado Oil then the Meatballs. Cook them for 15-20 minutes making sure to flip every 4-5 minutes to ensure a good sear on all sides.
5. Once you have seared your meatballs, remove from skillet and place them in a medium mixing bowl then set aside to prepare Homemade BBQ sauce.

6. In a 3 qt pot on medium heat, melt 3 tbsp of Butter. Once melted, add in Ketchup, Mustard, Worcestershire Sauce, White Distilled Vinegar, Mike's Hot Honey, Pineapple Juice, Brown Sugar, White Pepper, Chili Powder, Roasted Ground Cumin, Garlic & Herb seasoning, and PS Texas BBQ Rodeo Rub then mix.
7. Allow the sauce to come to a simmer then remove it from the heat. Pour half of the BBQ sauce over the Meatballs and save the other half for later. Give the Meatballs and the sauce a good toss in the mixing bowl then set aside.

GARLIC BUTTER STEAK LETTUCE BOATS

 4 Servings   Recipe   20 Minutes

INGREDIENTS:
- (2) Thick Cut NY Strip Steaks, Cubed
- (5) Garlic Cloves, Minced
- (1) Sweet Onion, Sliced
- (1) Lemon, Freshly Squeezed
- (1) Romaine Lettuce Head Fresh Parsley, Chopped Colby Jack Cheese, Shredded
- 6 tbsp Kerry Gold Garlic & Herb Butter
- 3 tbsp Avocado Oil
- 1/2 cup A1 Steak Sauce
- 1/4 cup Honey

SEASONINGS:
- 3 tsp Spiceology Rosemary Dijon Seasoning
- 3 tsp Spiceology Pink Peppercorn Lemon Thyme Seasoning
- 2 tsp McCormicks Roasted Garlic & Herb Seasoning

DIRECTIONS:
1. Remove Steaks from its package and pat dry as much moisture that maybe on the steak. Cut your Steak into cubes and place in a medium size mixing bowl for seasoning.
2. Combine the following seasoning with your cubed steak: Spiceology Rosemary Dijon Seasoning and Spiceology Pink Peppercorn Lemon Thyme Seasoning then message ingredients into the steak.
3. Into a large skillet on medium/high heat, pour in Avocado Oil along with the seasoned Steak bites. Cook the Steak for 3-5 minutes on each side or until brown.
4. Once Steak Bites have finished, reduce heat to medium/low and add in 4 tbsp of Garlic & Herb Butter, minced Garlic, and Freshly Chopped Parsley.
5. Mix ingredients together and allow your steak bites to simmer in the sauce for 2-3 minutes and then remove the Steak from the skillet into a mix bowl.

6. In that same skillet on medium heat, add in sliced Sweet Onions and saute them for 3-5 minutes or until translucent. Then remove them from the skillet to prepare sauce.

7. Clean out the skillet and turn the heat to a low temperature. Melt 2 tbsp of Garlic & Herb Butter and once melted add in A1 Steak Sauce, Honey, McCormicks Roasted Garlic & Herb Seasoning and freshly squeezed Lemon Juice. Turn the heat off on your sauce then mix until well combined.

8. Rinse off the Romaine Lettuce Head in cool water and cut the core off the bottom of it then begin separating the leaves from the main stem. These will serve as the Lettuce Boats.

9. Begin assembling your Lettuce boats with sauce first on the leaves, then the Steak, Sauteed Sweet Onions next, Shredded Colby Jack Cheese and finally more sauce to top it off and ENJOY!!

SALMON CAESAR LETTUCE BOATS

 4 Servings   Recipe   30 Minutes

INGREDIENTS:

- 1.5 lbs Atlantic Salmon
- 1 Romaine Lettuce Head
- 5 Garlic Cloves
- 4 Cento Rolled Anchovies
- 2 tbsp Fresh Lemon Juice
- 2 tbsp Worcestershire Sauce 2 tbsp Grey Poupon Dijon Mustard
- 2 tbsp Red Wine Vinegar
- 5 tbsp Mayo of choice
- 1 cup Olive Oil
- 1/2 cup Grated Parmesan Cheese

SEASONINGS:

- 2 tsp Kinder's Cracked Pepper Parmesan seasoning
- 2 tsp Kinder's Lemon Butter Garlic seasoning
- 2 tsp Old Bay seasoning
- 2 tsp Smoked Paprika
- 1 tsp Osmo White Flakey Salt
- 1 tsp Fresh Cracked Black Pepper

DIRECTIONS:

1. Preheat oven to 375
2. Remove Salmon from package. Depending on how you want to prepare your salmon, either cut into fillets or keep the salmon whole before moving to the next step.
3. Next, Pour on three tablespoons of Olive Oil over salmon, then season with Kinder's Cracked Pepper Parmesan seasoning, Kinder's Lemon Butter Garlic seasoning, Old Bay seasoning, and Smoked Paprika.
4. In a skillet on medium/high heat, pour in three tablespoons of Olive Oil, making sure it covers the bottom of the skillet. Place in Salmon in the skillet then sear the salmon on each side for 3-5 minutes depending on the size of the salmon.
5. Remember that you are only searing the salmon and not cooking it all the way through. Once you have a good sear on each side, remove the salmon from the skillet and onto a lined baking sheet.

6. Place the baking sheet into the oven to finish cooking the salmon. Bake the salmon the 10-12 minutes or until it reaches an internal temp of 145 degrees. Once the salmon is finished cooking, remove it from the oven and set aside.

7. Next, remove the stalk from Romaine Lettuce head then separate the leaves and place them in a large strainer. Run cool water over lettuce leaves to clean and keep them from softening. Remove them from the water and place on a napkin lined baking sheet then set aside to prepare Homemade Caesar Dressing.

HOMEMADE CAESAR DRESSING

1. Into a food processor or blender, add Garlic Cloves, Cento Rolled Anchovies, Worcestershire Sauce, French's Stone Ground Dijon Mustard, Mayo of choice, half cup of Olive Oil, freshly grated Parmesan Cheese, Osmo White Flakey Salt, fresh Cracked Black Pepper.

2. Blend for 2-3 minutes to give ingredients a good mix then build your Salmon Caesar Lettuce Boats. ENJOY!

POPCORN LOBSTER BITES

 4 Servings   Recipe   25 Minutes

INGREDIENTS:
- (2) Jumbo Lobster Tails
- 2 tbsp Mustard
- 3 tbsp Honey (FOR SAUCE)
- 4 tbsp Kerry Gold Garlic & Herb Butter (FOR SAUCE)
- 1 cup Franks Red Hot Sauce
- 2 cups Lefty's Spices Flour Mix
- 3 cups Peanut Cooking Oil

SEASONINGS:
- 1 tsp Garlic Herb Lemon Pepper Seasoning
- 1 tsp Cajun Seasoning
- 1 tsp Kingsford Garlic & Herb Seasoning
- 4 tsp Hidden Valley Ranch Seasoning

DIRECTIONS:
1. Remove the Lobster Tails from the package, grab a pair of shears, and cut the tops open. Pull the lobster meat, then cut it into cubes.
2. Next, place the lobster meat into a mixing bowl, then season it with garlic, herb, lemon pepper seasoning, and cajun seasoning. Then hit it with a bit of Mustard and mix.
3. In a medium mixing bowl, add a few cups of Lefty's Spices Flour Mix and two teaspoons of Hidden Valley Ranch seasoning, then mix.
4. Add the lobster meat to the flour mix and shake until they are fully coated, then sit aside to prepare cooking oil.
5. Bring 3 cups of Peanut Cooking Oil to 350 degrees. Add the lobster bites once the oil is ready, but DO NOT crowd the pot.
6. Fry the lobster bites for 2-4 minutes or until golden brown. Once the bites have finished cooking, remove them from the oil and place them on a wire rack to drain off any extra oil.

HOMEMADE HOT HONEY SAUCE

1. In a medium saucepan, melt 4 tbsp of Kerry Gold Garlic & Herb Butter. Once melted, pour in Franks Red Hot Sauce and honey, season with two teaspoons of Hidden Valley Ranch Seasoning and a little Kingsford Garlic & Herb Seasoning, then mix.
2. Reduce the heat to low and bring your sauce to a nice simmer. Allow the sauce to simmer briefly before removing it from the heat.
3. Add Lobster Bites to a serving bowl, pour the sauce over them, or have it on the side as a dipping sauce, and ENJOY!

BACON-WRAPPED CHICKEN BITES

 4 Servings   Recipe   🍲 1 Hour 15 Minutes

INGREDIENTS:

- (2) Boneless Chicken Breast
- 2 lbs Godshall's Beef Bacon
- 1 Stick Butter, Salted
- 3 tbsp Worcestershire Sauce
- 3 tbsp White Distilled Vinegar
- 3 tbsp Mike's Hot Honey
- 4 tbsp Avocado Oil
- 1 cup Ketchup
- 1/2 cup Mustard
- 1/4 cup Pineapple Mango Juice

SEASONINGS:

- 2 tbsp Hidden Valley Spicy Ranch Seasoning
- 4 tbsp BBQ Seasoning
- 4 tsp Chili Powder
- 2 tsp White Pepper
- 2 tsp Roasted Ground Cumin
- 2/3 cups Brown Sugar

DIRECTIONS:

1. Preheat oven to 350 degrees
2. Remove the Chicken Breast from the package, then dice them into medium-sized chunks. Place the chunks in a medium mixing bowl for seasoning.
3. Season the chicken with 2 tbsp of BBQ Seasoning, Hidden Valley Spicy Ranch Seasoning, then mix until each piece is fully seasoned.
4. Remove the Bacon strips from the package, then cut them in half. Take the chicken bites and roll them as tight as you can in one of the strips of bacon. Close off the ends with toothpicks and place them on a wire rack.
5. Add about 4 tbsp of Brown Sugar in a small ramekin and 2 tsp of Chili Powder, then mix. Sprinkle this seasoning mix over the wrapped chicken bites, then set aside to prepare Homemade BBQ sauce.
6. In a small pot on medium heat, melt 4 tbsp of Butter. Once melted, add in Ketchup, Mustard, Worcestershire Sauce, White Distilled Vinegar, Mike's Hot Honey, Pineapple Mango Juice, Brown Sugar, White Pepper, Chili Powder, Roasted Ground Cumin, and 2 tbsp of BBQ Seasonings, then mix.

7. Allow the sauce to simmer, then remove it from the heat. Dab the sauce on each wrapped chicken bite, ensuring the tops are nice and covered with the sauce.
8. Place the tray of chicken bites into the oven to cook for an hour. Halfway through the cooking process, flip the chicken bites, dab more of the BBQ sauce on the other side, then place back in the oven for 30-45 minutes or until the chicken reaches an internal temperature of 165 degrees.
9. Once complete, remove them from the oven, add a couple to a plate with some of that Homemade BBQ Sauce, and ENJOY!

FRIED SALMON BITES

 4 Servings   Recipe   15 Minutes

INGREDIENTS:
- 2 lb Atlantic Salmon
- 5 tbsp Mustard
- 4 tbsp Grated Parmesan Cheese
- 3 tbsp Butter
- 2 tbsp Minced Garlic
- 2 tbsp Minced Shallots
- 1 cup Lefty's Spiced Flour mix or your choice of AP Flour
- 2 cups Heavy Cream

SEASONINGS:
- 1 tsp OSMO White Flakey Salt
- 1 tsp Black Pepper
- 2 tsp Parsley
- 2 tsp Old Bay Seasoning
- 3 tsp Spice Theory Garlic Herb Pepper Blend
- 3 tsp Smoked Paprika

DIRECTIONS:
1. Preheat your choice of cooking oil to 350 degrees.
2. Remove Salmon from the package and pat dry any moisture to ensure seasonings will stick. Cut Salmon into strips, then dice into 2-inch chunks.
3. Add the Salmon chunks to a mixing bowl along with Mustard. Mustard is a great binder for seasonings when frying food and NO you don't taste the mustard after the frying process but it does boost the flavor!
4. Season the Salmon with Spice Theory Garlic Herb Pepper Blend and smoked Paprika then hand-mix the Salmon bites carefully so they don't break apart.
5. Pour in Lefty's Spice Flour or your choice of flour. Place a lid on top and give it a shake until the bites have all been coated with the flour evenly.
6. Begin dropping your bites into the preheated cooking oil. Be sure to not over fill the cooking oil with the bites, just a few at a time for an even fry for the salmon.

7. Only cook then in the cooking for for 2-3 minutes then check to make sure they have an internal temperature of 145 degrees.
8. Once finished, remove from oil and place them on a wire rack to cool and drain off any extra oil left behind then set aside to make a Seafood Cream Sauce.
9. In a medium saucepan on low heat, melt a couple tablespoons of Butter. Once half-way melted, being adding in Minced Garlic and Shallots, then sauté them for 2-4 minutes just until translucent then pour in Heavy Cream along with Old Bay seasoning, OSMO White Flakey Salt, Black Pepper, Parsley, and grated Parmesan Cheese then mix.
10. Allow your cream sauce to come to a simmer for 5 minutes before removing it from the heat, then grab a bowl of mash potatoes or grits and pour that delicious Seafood Cream Sauce over your Salmon Bites and ENJOY!

MAIN COURSES

BAKED ZITI

 5 Servings   Recipe   45 Minutes

INGREDIENTS:
- 1lb Ground Turkey
- 1lb Hatfield Ground Hot Italian Sausage
- 1 can Cento Crushed Tomatoes
- 1 White Onion, Diced
- 5 Garlic Cloves, Minced
- 1 cup Mozzarella Cheese, Shredded
- 1 cup American Cheese, Shredded
- 2 cups Spinach
- 3 cups Ziti Rigatoni Noddle's
- 3 cups Water
- 3 tbsp Olive Oil
- 1 tbsp Tomato Paste

SEASONINGS:
- 2 tbsp Italian Seasoning
- 2 tbsp Onion Powder
- 2 tbsp Garlic Powder
- 4 tbsp Salt
- 1 tbsp Basil
- 1 tbsp Oregano
- 1 tbsp White Sugar

DIRECTIONS:
1. Preheat oven to 375 degrees.
2. In a large skillet on medium heat, pour in some Olive Oil and allow the skillet to get nice and hot. Once ready add in Ground Turkey and Ground Hot Italian Sausage.
3. Cook your ground meat mixture until it begins to be brown. This process can take 10-15 minutes while you are mixing and breaking down your ground meat mixture into smaller chunks.
4. Once meat has browned add in diced White Onions, minced Garlic, and Spinach. Mix veggies into meat mixture until well combined.
5. Next, add in Tomato Paste along with a can of Crushed Red Tomatoes. Mix all ingredients until well combined then its time to season.
6. To your meat sauce you want to add the following seasoning: Italian Seasoning, Onion Powder, Garlic Powder, 2 tbsp Salt, Basil, Oregano, and White Sugar. Stir in seasonings until well combine with sauce. You can also season to taste as well.

7. Bring 3 cups of water and 2 tbsp of Salt to a boil on medium/high heat in a medium boiling pot. Once water is boiling reduce heat to medium/low and add in Ziti Rigatoni Noodle's. Allow noodles to cook for 8-10 minutes then remove from heat and drain water.

8. Grab a Pirex Dish or oven safe dish and for this next step it can be done many ways. You can layer your Ziti like you would Lasagna or mix noodles with meat sauce along with your mozzarella cheese and american cheese, either way is correct!

9. Once you have gotten your Ziti into the dish, cover with foil and its time to bake it. Place dish into preheated oven for 20 minutes. After time passes, remove foil and place dish back in for 10 more minutes to allow cheese to brown on top.

10. When the timer ends its time to begin eating! Remove dish from oven, garnish with a little parsley if you have it and DIG END!!

TARRAGON CHICKEN

 4 Servings   Recipe   30 Minutes

INGREDIENTS:
- 1 lb Thin Sliced Chicken Breast
- (2) Banana Shallots, Sliced
- Lemon Juice, Freshly Squeezed
- Lemon Zest
- Fresh Tarragon, Chopped
- 4 tbsp Delallo's Garlic & Herb Oil
- 1 cups Heavy Cream
- 1 cup Dark Horse Pinot Grigio

SEASONINGS:
- 4 tsp Badia Poultry Seasoning
- 4 tsp McCormick Roasted Garlic & Herb Seasoning
- 4 tsp Smoked Paprika
- 3 tbsp Mr. Make It Happen All-Purpose Seasoning

DIRECTIONS:
1. Rinse Chicken Breasts under cool water, then pat dry and place them in a medium mixing bowl for seasoning.
2. Season chicken with Badia Poultry Seasoning, McCormick Roasted Garlic & Herb Seasoning, and Smoked Paprika then massage in ingredients ensuring a good coating on each side.
3. In a 12-inch cast iron skillet on medium/high heat, pour in Delallo's Garlic & Herb Oil then add chicken breast. Cook them on each side for 4-6 minutes or until the internal temperature reaches 165 degrees.
4. Once the Chicken has finished, remove them from the skillet, then place them on a wire rack to cool and set aside to prepare sauce!
5. In the same skillet you just made the Chicken, reduce the heat to low and add in the sliced Banana Shallots. Saute the Shallots for 2-3 minutes then deglaze the skillet with some Dark Horse Pinot Grigio.

6. Next, pour in Heavy Cream along with a little Mr. Make It Happen All-Purpose Seasoning, Lemon Zest, freshly squeezed Lemon Juice and freshly chopped Tarragon.
7. Mix until well combined then bring sauce to a simmer. Once it simmers, turn off the heat then sit aside for a second to slice the Chicken breasts.
8. Afterwards, add some Homemade Garlic Mash Potatoes to a bowl then lay sliced Chicken Breast on top. Pour some of your Tarragon Sauce over the Chicken and Potatoes. Garnish with some Parsley and ENJOY!

STEAK ALFREDO

 3 Servings   Recipe   35 Minutes

INGREDIENTS:
- (2) New York Strip Steaks
- (1) Box Fettuccine Noodles
- (3) Garlic Cloves, peeled
- (2) Fresh Rosemary stems
- (1) 6 oz Bottle Sutter Home Pinot Grigio
- 2 tbsp Minced Garlic
- 2 tbsp Minced Shallots
- 6 tbsp Butter (SALTED)
- 4 tbsp Avocado Oil
- 1/2 cup Parmesan Cheese, Shredded
- 1.5 cups Heavy Cream
- 2 cups Broccoli Florets

SEASONINGS:
- 4 tsp Delallo's Rosemary Garlic Seasoning
- 3 tsp OSMO White Flakey Salt
- 3 tsp Kingsford Garlic & Herb Seasoning
- 3 tsp All-Purpose Seasoning
- 2 tsp Black Pepper

DIRECTIONS:
1. Remove steaks from the package, and lay the Steaks on a non-stick baking sheet. Pat the Steaks dry, then season them with Delallo's Rosemary Garlic Seasoning on both sides.
2. In a 12-inch skillet on medium/high heat, pour in a little Avocado Oil and lay the Steaks in once the skillet is nice and hot. Sear the Steaks for 3-6 minutes on each side, depending on how you like your steak. (This timeframe is for folks who enjoy Medium Rare, Medium, or Medium Well Done Steaks.)
3. After you flip the Steaks for the first time, add 2 tbsp of Butter, Garlic Cloves, and Rosemary stems. Once the butter has melted and infused with the garlic and rosemary, base the Steaks with the butter.
4. Once complete, remove the steaks from the skillet, place them on a wire rack, pour the rest of that infused butter over the Steaks, and then allow them to rest.
5. Bring 3 cups of water along with OSMO White Flakey Salt to a boil in a medium boiling pot. Once water is boiling, add one box of Fettuccine

Noodles, then reduce heat to medium and cook noodles for 11-12 minutes or until aldente.

6. Once the pasta is complete, turn off the heat, drain off the water, and sit aside to prepare veggies and alfredo sauce.

7. In a 10-inch skillet on medium heat, melt 2 tbsp of Butter. Once the butter has melted, add Minced Garlic and Minced Shallots, then, saute them for 1-2 minutes before adding in Broccoli Florets.

8. Add the Broccoli Florets after a couple minutes, season veggies with Kingsford Garlic and herb Seasoning, then saute them for 4-5 minutes before adding Pinot Grigio white wine. Pour in Pinot Grigio and allow it to reduce into your veggies.

9. Next, reduce heat to medium/low heat and pour in Heavy Cream, All-Purpose Seasoning, Black Pepper, and Parmesan Cheese, then allow the sauce to come to a simmer.

10. Once it has started simmering, turn off the heat and check to see if it is the right consistency you like, then add Fettuccine Noodles to the skillet with the sauce.

11. Give your pasta a good toss in that sauce, then slice the Steaks and lay them on top of that delicious pasta. Top off your pasta with shredded parmesan cheese, more pasta sauce, and parsley for garnish, then ENJOY!

STEAK ALFREDO FRENCH BREAD ZA

 4 Servings   Recipe 25 Minutes

INGREDIENTS:
- (2) New York Strip Steaks
- (1) French Bread Loaf
- (1) Stick Kerry Gold Garlic & Herb Butter
- 2 tbsp Minced Garlic
- 2 tbsp Minced Shallots
- 2 tbsp Parsley
- 2 tbsp Butter
- 2 tbsp Avocado Oil
- 1/2 cup Parmesan Cheese, Shredded
- 1/2 cup Mozzarella Cheese, Shredded
- 2 cups Heavy Cream
- 2 cups Spinach

SEASONINGS:
- 2 tsp Spice King Grilled Steak & Burger seasoning
- 2 tsp Simply Spice Garlic & Herb seasoning
- 2 tsp OSMO White Flakey Salt
- 2 tsp Smoke Paprika
- 2 tsp Cajun seasoning
- 2 tsp Black Pepper

DIRECTIONS:
1. Preheat oven to 350 degrees.
2. Begin by removing the steaks from the package and cutting them into 1-inch cubes, then place them into a mixing bowl.
3. In a 12-inch skillet on medium/high heat, pour some Avocado Oil and Steak cubes. Season the Steaks with Spice King Grilled Steak & Burger and Simply Spice Garlic Herb seasoning. Sear the steak cubes for 1-2 minutes, remove them from the skillet, and put them back into the mixing bowl. Set them aside to prepare the sauce.
4. After removing the steaks from the skillet, drop the heat to low and melt a couple of tablespoons of butter. Once melted, begin adding in mined Garlic and Shallots.
5. Sauté the garlic and shallots for a few minutes, then add in Heavy Cream along with the seasonings: OSMO White Flakey Salt, Black Pepper, Cajun seasoning, Parmesan Cheese, Parsley, and Smoked Paprika, then mix.

6. Allow the sauce to come to a simmer by raising the heat a little, and once it has started simmering for 2-4 minutes, turn off the heat and check to see if it is the right consistency you like, then set aside.

7. Grab your loaf of French Bread; half of it will do, depending on how much you are eating/serving then. Once you have the size you want for this Za, split the bread as if to make a sandwich. Lay it out on a lined baking sheet.

8. Smear on some Kerry Gold Garlic & Herb butter onto each slice of French Bread, then pour some of the Homemade Alfredo Sauce there next. Follow that by adding the Steak bites and then some fresh Spinach. Top it with more sauce, shredded Mozzarella Cheese, Parmesan Cheese, and Parsley.

9. Place the baking sheet into the oven for 5-10 minutes or until the Cheese melts on top. Once done, remove them from the oven, cut them into shareable pieces if you choose, and ENJOY!

CREAMY TOMATO RIGATONI

 2 Servings   Recipe   45 Minutes

INGREDIENTS:
- 7 On the vine Red Tomatoes
- 2 Garlic Bulbs
- 1 White Onion
- 1/2 cup Chicken Broth
- 1/2 cup Extra Virgin Olive Oil
- 1/4 cup Heavy Cream
- 1/4 cup Parmesan Cheese, Shredded
- 1 tbsp Tomato Paste

SEASONINGS:
- 2 tbsp Italian Seasoning
- 1 tbsp White Sugar
- 4 tsp OSMO White Flakey Salt
- 2 tsp Delallo's Sun-Dried Tomato & Basil Seasoning
- 2 tsp Delallo's Garlic & Tomato Seasoning

DIRECTIONS:
1. Preheat oven to 400 degrees.
2. Rinse Tomatoes under cool water, then grab a cutting board and begin slicing Tomatoes in half. Next, you want to peel and chop White Onion into chunks and cut the tops off the Garlic Bulbs.
3. Grab either a deep baking dish or a pyrex glass dish, then start adding your vegetable to the baking dish. Pour Extra Virgin Olive Oil over vegetables, then season with 2 tsp of OSMO White Flakey Salt and Italian Seasoning.
4. Place the baking dish uncovered in the oven, and you want to roast vegetables for 40 minutes. Once complete, remove the baking dish from the oven.
5. Into a blender of your choice, add in your roasted vegetables along with the Olive Oil that is at the bottom of the dish, then blend for 2-3 minutes or until you see a nice consistency. In a one qt sauce pot on low heat, pour in your blended Tomato Bisque.

6. Next, add Chicken Broth, Heavy Cream, Tomato Paste, Shredded Parmesan Cheese, Delallo's Sun-Dried Tomato & Basil Seasoning, Delallo's Garlic & Tomato Seasoning, White Sugar, and the other 2 tsp of OSMO White Flakey Salt, then mix.
7. Simmer your Tomato Bisque for 5 minutes on low heat. Once complete, grab a bowl, pour some in, and serve with a delicious Grilled Cheese and ENJOY!!

CREAMY JAMBALAYA PASTA

 4 Servings   *Recipe*   *35 Minutes*

INGREDIENTS:

- (1) Box Mafaldine Noodles
- (1) Red Bell Pepper, Sliced
- (1) Green Bell Pepper, Sliced
- (1) Sweet Onion, Sliced
- (1) Stick KerryGold Garlic & Herb Butter
- Beef Smoked Sausage, Sliced
- 8 oz Jumbo Lump Crab Meat
- 3 tbsp Minced Garlic
- 4 tbsp Avocado Oil
- 2 tbsp Tomato Paste
- 1/2 cup Parmesan Cheese, Shredded
- 2 cups Heavy Cream

SEASONINGS:

- 3 tsp Cajun Seasoning
- 3 tsp Creole Seasoning
- 3 tsp Garlic, Herb & Lemon Seasoning
- 3 tsp All-Purpose Seasoning
- 2 tsp Black Pepper

DIRECTIONS:

1. Clean Devein, remove the shells from the Shrimp, then pat dry and sit aside. Remove Smoked Sausage from its package, then slice into quarter pieces.

2. In a 12-inch skillet on medium/high heat, pour 2 tbsp of Avocado Oil and cook the Smoked Sausage first. Cook them for 3-5 minutes on each side, until they have a nice char on them, then remove from the skillet.

3. In that same skillet, add the Shrimp to the skillet, then season with Garlic, Herb, and lemon Seasoning and cook for 2-3 minutes on each side; remove them from the skillet and sit aside.

4. To that same skillet, add the Jumbo Lump Crab Meat with 2 tbsp of Garlic and herb Butter and saute the crab meat for 2-3 minutes, then remove from the skillet and set aside.

5. Bring 3 cups of water to a boil in a medium boiling pot. Once water is boiling, add one box of Mafaldine Noodles, then reduce heat to medium and cook noodles for 11-12 minutes or until aldente.

6. Once the pasta is complete, turn off the heat, drain off the water, and set aside to prepare veggies and the sauce.
7. In a 10-inch skillet on medium heat, pour 2 tbsp of Avocado Oil. Once the oil is ready, add Minced Garlic, Sliced Red, Green Pepper, and Onions. Seasoning veggies with All-Purpose seasoning, then saute them for 3-5 minutes.
8. Next, add Tomato Paste with 2 tbsp of Kerrygold Garlic and herb Butter, then mix into veggies until the butter melts.
9. Reduce the heat to medium/low heat and pour in the Heavy Cream. Season your sauce with Creole Seasoning, Black Pepper, Cajun Seasoning, and Parmesan Cheese, then mix until well combined. Allow the sauce to simmer, then reduce the heat to low.
10. Once the sauce is consistent, shut off the heat and add the Mafaldine Noodles to the skillet with the sauce and veggies.
11. Give your pasta a good toss in that sauce, then add the Smoked Sausage, Shrimp, and Crab Meat to the top of the pasta. Top off your pasta with shredded parmesan cheese, more pasta sauce, and parsley for garnish, then ENJOY!

CREAMY GARLIC LEMON PASTA

 3 Servings   Recipe   30 Minutes

INGREDIENTS:

- 1 Box Mafaldine Noodles
- Lemon Zest, Fresh Lemon
- 1/2 Fresh Lemon, Juiced
- Fresh Parsley, Chopped
- 2 tbsp Garlic Paste
- 3 tbsp Butter
- 2 tbsp Avocado Oil
- 1/4 cup White Onions, Chopped
- 1/2 cup Parmesan Cheese, Shredded
- 1/2 cup Shutter Home Pinot Grigio Wine
- 1 cup Heavy Cream
- 3-4 cups of Water

SEASONINGS:

- 2 tsp Crushed Red Pepper Flakes
- 2 tsp OSMO White Flakey Salt
- 2 tsp Black Pepper
- 4 tsp Kingsford Garlic & Herbs Seasoning

DIRECTIONS:

1. In a medium crock pot, add 3-4 cups of water and OSMO White Flakey Salt. Turn your heat to medium/high to bring water to a boil. Once water is boiling, add 1 Box of Mafaldine Noodles, then reduce heat to medium and cook noodles for 9-12 minutes or until aldente. Once the noodles have finished cooking, drain them of the water and sit aside to create the sauce.
2. In a medium skillet on low heat, add Avocado Oil, Garlic Paste and chopped White Onions then saute onions and garlic for 3-4 minutes.
3. Pour in 6oz Shutter Home Pinot Grigio Wine to deglaze the skillet then add fresh Lemon Zest along with freshly squeezed Lemon Juice.
4. Next, pour in Heavy Cream then season with Kingsford Garlic & Herbs Seasoning, Black Pepper, Crushed Red Pepper Flakes, and shredded Parmesan Cheese then until well combined.
5. Allow your sauce to come to a simmer and once it does, turn off the heat then add the pasta noodles to the sauce and mix

6. Grab a bowl and fill it with your Creamy noodles. Spinkle on a little more Parmesan cheese then ENJOY!

CREAMY CHICKEN PESTO PASTA

 3 Servings   Recipe   45 Minutes

INGREDIENTS:
- (1) Box Mafaldine Noodles
- (3) Chicken Breast
- (3) Garlic Knots
- (6) Cherry Tomatoes, Sliced
- 2 oz Pine Nuts
- Fresh Basil
- 1/2 Fresh Lemon, Juiced
- Fresh Parsley, Chopped
- 3 tbsp Minced Garlic
- 3 tbsp Minced Shallot
- 4 tbsp Garlic & Herb Butter
- 8 tbsp Olive Oil
- 2 cups Fresh Spinach
- 1/2 cup Parmesan Cheese, Shredded
- 1 cup Heavy Cream
- 3-4 cups of Water

SEASONINGS:
- 3 tsp Cajun Seasoning
- 3 tsp Rosemary Garlic Seasoning
- 7 tsp Salt
- 2 tsp All-Purpose Seasoning

DIRECTIONS:
1. Preheat oven to 375 degrees.
2. Remove the Chicken Breast from the package and clean the breast in lemons and vinegar. Once finished, pat the breast dry and place in a large mixing bowl.
3. Into the bowl, pour in 3 tbsp Olive oil, Cajun Seasoning, and Rosemary Garlic Seasoning. Massage ingredients into the breast on both sides.
4. In a 12-inch skillet on high heat, pour in 3 tbsp Olive Oil, then the Chicken Breast. Sear the chicken breast for 5-7 minutes on both sides.
5. Once you have a good sear on each side, remove the breast from the skillet and place them on a wire rack. Place the Chicken breasts in the oven for 15-20 minutes or until they reach an internal temperature of 160 degrees, then remove them from the oven and set aside.
6. In a medium pot, add 3-4 cups of water and 2 tsp Salt. Turn your heat to medium/high to bring water to a boil.

7. Once water is boiling, add 1 Box of Mafaldine Noodles, then reduce heat to medium and cook noodles for 9-12 minutes or until aldente. After the noodles have finished cooking, drain them of the water and sit aside to prepare Homemade Pesto Sauce.

8. In a food processor or blender, add Pine Nuts, 2 tsp Salt, Fresh Basil, Garlic Cloves, grated Parmesan Cheese, AP Seasoning, and 2 tbsp Olive Oil. Blend until you get to your desired consistency.

9. In a large skillet on medium heat, melt half a stick of Garlic and herb Butter, and once it has just about softened, throw in some diced Garlic and Shallots, then saute them for 3-4 minutes in that delicious butter.

10. After they have sauteed for a bit, add some Lemon Juice, a couple of cups of Spinach, and sliced Cherry Tomatoes. Once the Spinach and Tomatoes have been cooked, pour in Heavy Cream, Parmesan Cheese, 3 tsp Salt, and a couple of tbsp of your Homemade Pesto sauce, then mix.

11. Allow your sauce to come to a simmer, and once it does, turn the heat to low, add the pasta noodles to the sauce, and mix until well combined, then turn off the heat completely.

12. At this time, slice down the Chicken Breast, add some of your delicious Pesto Pasta to a bowl with the sliced chicken on top, and ENJOY!

CREAMY SHRIMP SCAMPI PASTA

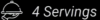 4 Servings   Recipe   30 Minutes

INGREDIENTS:
- 2 lbs. Extra Jumbo Shrimp
- (1) Box Barilla Linguine Noodles
- 1/2 Fresh Lemon, Juiced
- 1/2 White Onion, Diced Fresh Parsley, Chopped
- 4 tbsp. Butter
- 4 tbsp. Olive Oil
- 2 tbsp. Minced Garlic
- 1/4 cup Entcy Infused White Wine
- 1/2 cup Freshly Chopped Parsley
- 1/2 Heavy Cream
- 1/2 cup Parmesan Cheese, Shredded
- 3-4 cups of Water

SEASONINGS:
- 2 tsp. Kinder's Cracked Lemon Pepper seasoning
- 2 tsp. Spiceology Black Magic Cajun seasoning
- 2 tsp. Nick's Brandied Pepper seasoning
- 1 tsp. Crushed Red Pepper Flakes

DIRECTIONS:
1. Rinse and peel the extra jumbo shrimp, then pat them dry, removing as much moisture as possible. Place the shrimp into a mixing bowl for seasoning.
2. Pour in two tablespoons of Olive Oil, then season the shrimp with Kinder's Cracked Lemon Pepper seasoning, Spiceology Cajun seasoning, and some freshly chopped Parsley. Mix.
3. In a medium pot on medium heat, bring 3-4 cups of water to a boil. Once the water begins to boil, salt it generously and add the box of Linguine Noodles. Boil the noodles for 12-15 minutes, drain off the water, and set aside.
4. Pour two tablespoons of olive oil into a skillet on medium/high heat. Once the skillet is ready, add the shrimp. Cook the shrimp for 2-3 minutes on each side, then cut the heat and remove them from the skillet.
5. Reduce the heat in the skillet to medium/low, then melt a couple of

tablespoons of Butter. Once melted, toss in some minced Garlic and diced onions.

6. Saute the onions and garlic for a few minutes, then add your choice of white wine and a few more tablespoons of butter. Allow the wine to reduce in the skillet, then pour a little Heavy Cream.

7. Season the sauce with Nick's Brandied Pepper seasoning, Crushed Red Pepper Flakes, some freshly shredded Parmesan Cheese, Lemon Zest from a fresh lemon along with the juice, and finally, some freshly chopped Parsley. Mix.

8. Bring the sauce to a simmer, and once it has reached a satisfactory consistency, drop the heat to low and add the pasta and shrimp to the sauce. Give everything a good mix, then garnish it with more shredded Parmesan cheese and fresh Parsley.

9. Grab a bowl or eat this straight out of the skillet, gang! ENJOY!.

CRAB STUFFED SALMON PASTA

 4 Servings   Recipe   45 Minutes

INGREDIENTS:

- 2 lbs Atlantic Salmon
- 16 oz Jumbo Lump Crab Meat
- 1 Box Penne Noodles
- 1 tsp Garlic Paste
- 2 tbsp Minced Shallots
- 2 tbsp Hot Sauce
- 3 tbsp Avocado Oil
- 3 tbsp Dijon Mustard
- 4 tbsp Kerry Gold Garlic & Herb Butter
- 1/4 cup RITZ Garlic Butter Crackers
- 1 cup Grated Parmesan Cheese
- 2 cups Heavy Cream
- 3 cups Water

SEASONINGS:

- 1 tsp Tony Chachere's Original Creole Seasoning
- 1 tsp Old Bay Garlic & Herb Seasoning
- 1 tsp Kinder's Cracked Lemon Pepper Seasoning
- 2 tsp Cajun Seasoning
- 3 tsp Simply Spice Garlic Herb Lemon Pepper Seasoning
- 3 tsp Smoked Paprika
- 4 tsp Black Pepper
- 4 tsp Parsley
  6 tsp OSMO White Flakey Salt

DIRECTIONS:

1. Preheat oven to 400.
2. Remove Salmon from the package, pat dry any moisture left behind for seasonings, then cut out 3-4 fillets.
3. Once the Salmon is cut into fillets, slice a 2-inch slit in the middle of salmon pieces for the Crab stuffing for later.
4. Next, pour some Avocado Oil over Salmon fillets then season them with Simply Spice Garlic Herb Lemon Pepper seasoning, Smoked Paprika, and 3 tsp of Black Pepper.
5. Be sure to rub seasoning in thoroughly including in the slit where the crab stuffing will sit.
6. In a medium mixing bowl, add in Dijon Mustard, Hot Sauce, Old Bay Garlic & Herb seasoning, Kinder's Cracked Lemon Pepper seasoning, Tony Chachere's Original Creole Seasoning, Parsley, and RITZ Garlic Butter crackers then mix until well combined.
7. Next, add the Jumbo Lump Crab meat to mixture and fold in crab meat DO NOT STIR. Once your crab mixture is ready, start stuffing your Salmon fillets.

8. Once the fillets stuffed, place the Salmon on a wire rack and put them into the oven to cook for 20-25 minutes or until the internal temparatue of the Salmon is at 145 degrees.
9. Remove your Crab Stuffed Salmon from the oven and sit aside to prepare pasta and the sauce.
10. Bring 3 cups of water along with OSMO White Flakey Salt to a boil in a medium boiling pot. Once water is boiling, add one box of Penne Noodles, then reduce heat to medium and cook noodles for 9-11 minutes or until aldente.
11. Once the pasta is complete, turn off the heat, drain off the water, and sit aside to prepare the sauce.
12. In a 12-inch skillet on medium heat, melt 4 tbsp of Kerry Gold Garlic & Herb Butter. Once the butter has melted, add in Minced Shallots and Garlic Paste. You want to saute them for 1-2 minutes before adding in the Heavy Cream.
13. Next, reduce heat to medium/low heat and pour in the Heavy Cream then seasoning the sauce with Cajun seasoning, 1 tsp Black Pepper, OSMO White Flakey Salt, Parsley and Grated Parmesan Cheese and mix.
14. Once the sauce has started simmering, check to see if it is the right consistency you like, cut off the heat and mix in the Penne Noodles with the sauce. Give your pasta a good toss in that sauce for 1-2 minutes to make sure all the ingredients are well combined.
15. Fill a couple bowls with your pasta along with one of the Crab Stuffed Salmon filets on top and ENJOY!

SPICY SHRIMP PASTA

 3-4 Servings   *Recipe*   *30 Minutes*

INGREDIENTS:
- 2 lb Extra Large Shrimp
- 1 Box Fettuccini Noodles
- 2 tbsp Fresh Parsley, Chopped
- 2 tbsp Garlic Paste
- 3 tbsp Fresh Lemon Juice
- 4 tbsp Olive Oil
- 4 tbsp Butter, Salted
- 4 cups Water
- 2 cups Heavy Cream
- 1 cup Broccoli Florets
- 1 cup Heavy Cream
- 1/2 cup Parmesan Cheese, Grated

SEASONINGS:
- 2 tbsp Weber Roasted Garlic & Herb Seasoning
- 2 tbsp Old Bay Lemon & Herb Seasoning
- 2 tbsp Kingsford's Garlic & Herb Seasoning
- 1 tbsp Smoked Paprika
- 2 tsp OSMO White Flakey Salt
- 2 tsp Black Pepper
- 2 tsp Crushed Red Pepper Flakes

DIRECTIONS:
1. Rinse off and peel your shrimp, then pat the shrimp dry, removing as much moisture as possible. Then, place the shrimp in a medium mixing bowl for seasoning.
2. Pour in Olive Oil and season with Weber Roasted Garlic & Herb Seasoning, Old Bay Lemon & Herb Seasoning, and Smoked Paprika, then mix until the shrimp is fully coated.
3. In a skillet on medium/high heat, pour in a tablespoon of Olive Oil and add the Shrimp. Cook the shrimp on each side for 3-4 minutes, then remove from skillet and set aside.
4. In the same skillet, melt a few tablespoons of salted Butter. Once the butter has melted, add the Broccoli along with some Kingsford's Garlic and herb seasoning. Sauté the Broccoli for 6-8 minutes on medium heat. Once they are done, remove them from the skillet and set aside.
5. In a 4qt boiling pot, bring 3-4 cups of water to a boil. Once the water is ready, generously salt the water and add the Fettuccini Noodles.

6. Cook the noodles for 10-12 minutes or until aldente, then drain the water while keeping some of the pasta water for your sauce later and set them aside.

7. Melt another couple of tablespoons of salted butter in a 12-inch skillet on medium/low heat. After the butter has melted, add some Garlic Paste, freshly squeezed Lemon Juice, some of the pasta water from earlier, and Heavy Cream.

8. Reduce the heat to low, then season the sauce with OSMO White Flakey Salt, Black Pepper, Crushed Red Pepper Flakes, grated Parmesan Cheese, and Parsley. Mix until well combined.

9. Allow your Homemade Alfredo sauce to come to a simmer. Once it does, add the Fettuccini Noodles, Broccoli, and Shrimp, then mix everything together.

10. Top it off with more Parmesan Cheese and Parsley and more of that delicious Homemade Alfredo sauce, and ENJOY!

MARRY ME SALMON PASTA

 4 Servings   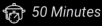 Recipe   50 Minutes

INGREDIENTS:
- (4) Skinless Salmon Fillets
- 2 tbsp Stir-In Chunky Garlic Paste
- 3 tbsp Kerry Gold Garlic & Herb Butter
- 8 tbsp Avocado Oil
- 2 tbsp Sun-Dried Tomatoes
- 1 tbsp Sun-Dried Tomato Oil
- 1 tbsp Tomato Paste
- 1/2 cup Parmesan Cheese
- 2 cups Baby Spinach
- 2 cups Girelle Pasta
- 1.5 cups Seafood Broth
- 1.5 cups Heavy Cream

SEASONINGS:
- 1 tbsp Crushed Red Pepper Flakes
- 6 tbsp OSMO White Flakey Salt
- 2 tbsp Smoked Paprika
- 2 tbsp Chicken Seasoning
- 2 tbsp Oregano
- 4 tbsp Thyme Leaves
- 4 tbsp Italian Seasoning

DIRECTIONS:
1. Remove the Salmon filets from the package, pat them dry, and lay them on a baking sheet for seasoning.
2. Pour 4 tbsp of Avocado Oil on the Salmon, then season them with Honey Garlic Chipotle Lime seasoning from Simply Spicy Spice. Massage the seasoning into the Salmon thoroughly on both sides.
3. Preheat a 12-inch cast iron skillet on medium/high heat. Once the skillet is ready, pour in 3 tbsp of Avocado Oil, then begin laying in the Salmon.
4. Sear the filets for 5-7 minutes on each side. After the first time you flip the Salmon, reduce the heat to a Medium/Low temperature, then throw in a couple tablespoons of Kerry Gold Garlic and Herb Butter.
5. Once the butter melts, baste the Salmon in the garlic butter, then continue to allow the Salmon to cook in the butter for 3-5 minutes or until they reach an internal temperature of 145 degrees.
6. After cooking, remove them from the skillet, place them on a wire rack, and set them aside to prepare the pasta and the cream sauce.

7. Bring 4 quarts of water to a boil on high heat, then add about 3 tbsp of OSMO White Flakey Salt to the water along with the Girelle Pasta.
8. Reduce the heat to Medium and cook the pasta for 14-16 minutes UNCOVERED. Once the pasta is done, turn off the heat, then drain the water from the pasta.
9. In a 10-inch skillet on Medium heat, pour in 2 tbsp of Avocado Oil along with Stir-In Chunky Garlic Paste, Baby Spinach, Tomato Paste, Sun Dried Tomatoes, some of the Oil from the Sun Dried Tomatoes, and All-Purpose seasoning by Simply Spicy Spice.
10. Saute everything for 5-7 minutes so the Spinach breaks down into the skillet evenly, then pour in Seafood Stock and Heavy Cream.
11. Next, season the sauce with Delallo's Sun-Dried Tomato and basil seasoning, Delallo's Garlic and tomato seasoning, Crushed Red Pepper Flakes, Black Pepper, 2 tbsp OSMO White Flakey Salt, and 1/4 cup grated Parmesan Cheese, then mix.
12. Allow the sauce to come to a simmer, then let it simmer for 4-6 minutes to get a little thick. Once the sauce has reached your desired consistency, turn off the heat and add the Girelle Pasta. Give everything a good mix together, then add the Salmon filets on top of the Salmon.
13. Pour more delicious sauce on the Salmon and Pasta, grab a fork, and eat straight out of the skillet. ENJOY!

MARRY ME STEAK PASTA

 2 Servings　　 *Recipe*　　 *30 Minutes*

INGREDIENTS:
- (2) Ribeye Steaks
- (5) Garlic Knots
- (8) Cherry Tomatoes
  Fresh Parsley
- Fresh Thyme
- 6 tbsp Butter, Salted
- 1/2 cup Parmesan
  Cheese
- 1 cup Chicken Broth
- 1 cup Heavy Cream

SEASONINGS:
- 2 tsp Black Pepper
  3 tsp Tabitha
  Brown's Very Good
  Garlic Seasoning
- 4 tsp OSMO White
  Flakey Salt
- 4 tsp KInder's
  Prime Steak
  Seasoning

DIRECTIONS:
1. Remove the Steaks from the package, pat them dry, and lay them on a baking sheet for seasoning. Season them with Kinder's Prime Steak seasoning on all sides, then set aside.
2. Preheat a 12-inch cast iron skillet on high heat, and once the skillet is ready, pour in a couple of tablespoons of Avocado Oil, then lay in the Steaks.
3. Sear the steaks for 3-5 minutes on each side. After the first flip, add Butter, Garlic Knots, and Thyme. Once the butter melts, baste the steaks for another 3-4 minutes then cut the heat and remove the steaks from the skillet and onto a wire rack to rest. Resting the steaks allows the juices to redistribute, resulting in a more tender and flavorful steak.
4. While the steaks are resting, this is the best time to prepare the Marry Me Sauce! In the same skillet, you just prepare the steaks on medium heat, adding minced garlic, shallots, and cherry tomatoes.

5. Season the veggies with Tabitha Brown's Very Good Garlic seasoning and saute them for 4 minutes. Then, pour in Heavy Cream and Chicken Broth. Season the sauce with some Osmo White Flakey Salt, Black Pepper, grated Parmesan Cheese, and freshly chopped Parsley, then mix until well combined.

6. Allow the sauce to come to a rolling simmer then drop the heat to low and begin slicing the steaks that have been resting. Add the steaks to the sauce, drizzle the sauce over the steak, then garnish with Parsley and have with your favorite sides! ENJOY!

SEAFOOD STUFFED PASTA SHELLS

 4 Servings   Recipe   60 Minutes

INGREDIENTS:

- 1.5 lb Raw Jumbo Shrimp
- 8 oz Jumbo Crab Meat
- (1) Box Jumbo Pasta Shells
- 3 tbsp Minced Garlic
- 3 tbsp Minced Shallots
- 8 tbsp Avocado Oil
- 1/2 cup Parmesan Cheese, Shredded
- 1/2 cup Mozzarella Cheese, Shredded
- 2 cups Heavy Cream
- 2 cups Spinach

SEASONINGS:

- 2 tsp Garlic Butter Seasoning
- 2 tsp Cajun Seasoning
- 4 tsp Osmo White Flaky Salt
- 4 tsp Smoked Paprika
- 1 tsp All-Purpose Seasoning
- 2 tsp Black Pepper

DIRECTIONS:

1. Preheat oven to 350 degrees.
2. Peel and devein the shrimp. Afterward, rinse them in cool water, pat them dry, and place them in a mixing bowl for seasoning.
3. Seasoning the Shrimp with McCormick Garlic Butter Seasoning and Cajun Seasoning along with 3 tbsp of Avocado Oil, then mix until well combined.
4. In a 12-inch skillet on medium/high heat, pour 3 tbsp of Avocado Oil and seasoned Shrimp once the skillet is nice and hot. Sear the Shrimp for 3 minutes on each side. Once complete, remove the Shrimp from the skillet, leaving the oil and seasonings behind. Cut the Shrimp in half to make it easier to stuff in the shells later.
5. Next, add the Jumbo Lump Crab meat to the skillet. Mix the Crab meat with the oil and seasonings from the skillet while on medium heat. Saute the Crab meat for 3-4 minutes, then remove from the skillet.
6. Add the Shrimp and Crab meat to a mixing bowl, and some shredded Parmesan Cheese, Mozzarella Cheese, and Parsley, then mix. This will be the stuffing for the Pasta Shells.

7. Bring 3 cups of water along with OSMO White Flakey Salt to a boil in a medium boiling pot. Once water is boiling, add one box of Jumbo Shells, then reduce heat to medium and cook noodles for 11-12 minutes or until aldente. Once the pasta is complete, turn off the heat, drain off the water, and set aside to prepare the alfredo sauce.
8. In a 10-inch skillet on medium heat, pour in 3 tbsp of Avocado Oil along with Minced Garlic, Shallots, and Spinach, then saute the veggies for 3-5 minutes before adding in the heavy cream.
9. Next, reduce heat to medium/low heat and pour in Heavy Cream, All-Purpose seasoning, Black Pepper, Parmesan Cheese, and Parsley, then allow the sauce to simmer.
10. Once it has started simmering, turn the heat on low, check to see if it is the right consistency you like, and then begin stuffing the Pasta Shells with the Seafood mix.
11. Grab a baking dish of your choosing, remove the sauce from the heat, and pour a little sauce into the baking dish. Just enough to cover the bottom of the dish.
12. Begin adding the Stuffed Shells to the baking dish. Once you fit as many in the baking dish, pour the rest of the Alfredo Sauce on top of the shells. Add some shredded Parmesan Cheese, Mozzarella Cheese, and Parsley to the top of the shells, then place them in the oven for 15-20 minutes.
13. Once complete, remove the baking dish from the oven, plate your delicious Seafood Pasta Shells with some garlic bread on the side, and ENJOY!

ALFREDO STUFFED CORNISH HENS

 2 Servings   *Recipe*   *1 Hour 50 Minutes*

INGREDIENTS:
- (2) Cornish Hens
- (1) Shallot, Minced
- (5) Garlic Cloves, Minced
- 1/2 cup Tony Chacheres Injectable Butter
- 1/2 cup Freshly Grated Parmesan Cheese
- 1/2 cup Freshly Chopped Parsley
- 1 cup Chicken Broth
- 2 cups Spinach
- 4 cups Water
- 4 tbsp Olive Oil

SEASONINGS:
- 1 tsp Granulated Chicken Seasoning
- 1 tsp Thyme Leave
- 2 tsp Badia Sazon Tropical Seasoning
- 2 tsp Kinder's Italian Chop House Seasoning
- 2 tsp Knder's Lemon Butter Garlic Seasoning
- 2 tsp Black Pepper
- 2 tsp Spice Theory Garlic Herb Pepper Blend
- 4 tsp Osmo White Flakey Salt

DIRECTIONS:
1. Preheat oven to 400 degrees.
2. Rinse off the Cornish Hens in cool water with fresh limes and vinegar if you have any. Remove any feathers on the Hens, then pat dry for the next step.
3. Place the Cornish Hens in a large mixing bowl, pour on some Olive Oil, and season with Badia Sazon Tropical seasoning, Kinder's Italian Chop House seasoning, Knder's Lemon Butter Garlic seasoning, and freshly chopped Parsley.
4. Message the ingredients into the Cornish Hens and pour some Tony Chacheres Injectable Butter into a medium ramekin. Take a syringe, gather a good amount of butter, and inject each Hen.
5. Next, add some chicken broth to a measuring cup, granulated chicken Bouillon seasoning, and thyme leaves, and then mix until well combined.
6. Pour this mixture into the bottom of the baking dish the Hens are in. DON'T completely submerge the Hens in the sauce; just enough to cover the bottom of the baking dish.

7. Place the dish in the oven uncovered for 1 hour and 20 minutes, or until the hens reach an internal temperature of 165 degrees. After every 20 minutes, baste the Hens in the juices from the bottom of the baking dish to ensure they do not burn.
8. While the Hens cook, it is time to prepare the alfredo sauce. In a 10-inch skillet on medium heat, melt a couple of tablespoons of butter.Once it melts, begin to saute the minced Garlic, Shallots, and Spinach.
9. Once the spinach has cooked, pour in some heavy cream and season it with two teaspoons of Osmo White Flake Salt, Black Pepper, and Spice Theory Garlic Herb Pepper seasoning, then mix.
10. Cut the heat, sprinkle in some freshly chopped Parsley, finish with some freshly grated Parmesan Cheese, and mix until well combined.
11. In a medium pot, bring 3 cups of water and a couple of teaspoons of Salt to a boil. Once the water is boiling, add one box of Penne Noodles, then reduce the heat to medium and cook the noodles for 11-13 minutes.
12. Toss the cooked Penne pasta into the sauce and mix! Now that the Alfredo has been made, it is time to stuff the Cornish Hens.
13. By this time, the Cornish Hens should be ready. Pull the Hens from the oven and place them into individual bowls. Take a pair of shears and cut right down the middle of the chest cavity of the hens. Split them and begin to add the Alfredo pasta in the middle! Sprinkle on some freshly chopped Parsley, finish with a little more freshly grated Parmesan Cheese, and ENJOY!

FRIED CORNISH HENS

 4 Servings   *Recipe*   *35 Minutes*

INGREDIENTS:

- 4 Cornish Hens
- 1/2 cup Mustard Fresh Rosemary Spriggs
- 3 tsp Cornstarch
- 3 cups Peanut Cooking Oil

SEASONINGS:

- 1/4 cup Garlic & Herb Seasoning
- 1/4 cup Cajun Seasoning

DIRECTIONS:

1. Remove the Cornish Hens from the package and place them in a large mixing bowl. You can clean them with lemons and limes or pat them dry and move to the next step.
2. Next, add Mustard as your binder, followed by your seasonings, Garlic & Herb Seasoning, Cajun Seasoning, and Cornstarch, then mix.
3. In a 5-quart pot on medium/high heat, pour Peanut Cooking Oil and a few Fresh Rosemary Spriggs. Once the oil reaches a temperature of 325, add the Cornish Hens two at a time to prevent overcrowding the pot.
4. Allow the Hens to cook for 16-18 minutes or until the internal temp reaches 165 degrees. Once the hens have finished cooking, remove them from the oil and place them on a wire rack to drain off the extra grease.
5. Grab a couple of plates, fill them with your favorite side dishes and your perfectly fried Cornish Hen, and ENJOY!

SALMON ALFREDO LASAGNA ROLLS

 3 Servings   Recipe   50 Minutes

INGREDIENTS:
- 1.5 lbs Salmon Fillet
- (6) Lasagna Noodles
- 1/2 Green Pepper, Diced
- 1/2 Red Pepper, Diced
- 1 tbsp Minced Garlic
- 2 tbsp Garlic & Herb Butter 4 tbsp Avocado Oil
- 1/2 cup Parmesan Cheese, Shredded
- 1/2 cup Mozzarella Cheese
- 1/2 cup Colby Cheese
- 2 cups Baby Spinach
- 2 cups Heavy Cream

SEASONINGS:
- 2 tsp All-Purpose Seasoning
- 2 tsp Kingsford Garlic & Herbs Seasoning
- 2 tsp Smoked Paprika
- 2 tsp Badia Complete Seasoning
- 2 tsp OSMO White Flakey Salt
- 2 tbsp Cajun Seasoning
- 1 tsp Black Pepper

DIRECTIONS:
1. Preheat oven to 350 degrees.
2. Remove Salmon from package then pour 2 tbsp of Avocado Oil along with All-Purpose Seasoning, Garlic & Herb Seasoning, and Smoked Paprika. Massage oil and seasonings into salmon then sit aside.
3. Preheat a 12-inch cast iron skillet on medium/high heat, once the skillet is ready, pour in 2 tbsp of Avocado Oil.
4. After the oil has coated the skillet, lay Salmon in and sear for 3-5 minutes on each side. After searing, remove the Salmon from the skillet and place it on a wire rack to rest while you prepare the sauce.
5. Clean out the skillet and reduce the heat in your skillet to medium heat, then add another 2 tbsp of Avocado Oil.
6. Next, add in Minced Garlic, diced Green and Red Peppers, Spinach and Badia Complete Seasoning then mix. Saute veggies for 3-5 minutes then pour in Heavy Cream and mix.

7. Allow the sauce to come to a simmer then season the sauce with Cajun Seasoning Black Pepper, OSMO White Flakey Salt, and stressed Parmesan Cheese. Turn off the heat and sit aside.
8. Boil 3 qts of water in a large boiling pot with salt then add in 6-7 Lasagna Noodles. Cook them for 10-12 minutes just until al dente. Once they have finished cooking, drain the water and lay them out an inch apart.
9. Begin layering noodles with Mozzarella Cheese first, then the Salmon, and then the Sauce. Next roll Lasagna noodles nice and tight.
10. Layer the bottom of a glass baking dish with more sauce then place the Lasagna Rolls in the baking dish, top them off with more of that delicious sauce and shredded Colby Cheese.
11. Place in preheated oven for 15-20 minutes, just long enough for the cheese to melt on top. Remove the dish from the oven and plate a couple Lasagna Rolls then ENJOY!!

GRILLED JERK SHORT RIBS

 3 Servings   Recipe   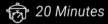 20 Minutes

INGREDIENTS:
- (2) 8oz Phillips Jumbo Lump Crab Meat
- (8) Egg Roll Wrappers
- 1 Egg
- 1/2 cup Mayo
- 1/4 cup Ritz Crackers
- 3 cups Cooking Oil
- 2 tbsp Fresh Squeezed Lemon Juice
- 1 tbsp Worcestershire Sauce
- 1 tbsp Grey Poupon Dijon Mustard
- 1 tbsp Stir-in Garlic Paste
- 2 tbsp Old Bay Seasoning

SEASONINGS:
- 1 tbsp Old Bay Seasoning
- 1 tbsp Onion Powder
- 1 tbsp Garlic Powder
- 1 tsp Black Pepper

DIRECTIONS:
1. Into a medium mixing bowl, combine the following ingredients: Mayo of choice, Grey Poupon Dijon Mustard, Worcestershire Sauce, Old Bay Seasoning, Onion Powder, Garlic Powder, Fresh Black Pepper, Freshly squeezed Lemon Juice, Garlic Paste and finally 1 Egg. Mix these ingredients until well combined.
2. Open your two packs of 8oz Phillips Crab meat, then add to your batter. Always remember to FOLD in crab meat and NEVER STIR.
3. After folding in batter, add 1/4 cup of Ritz Cracker crumbles to hold crab cake stuffing in shape for egg rolls. Lay out egg roll wrappers and add your crab cake stuffing to the wraps. Fold in the ends, then wrap. Dab a little water to the wrap's ends to help close the egg rolls.
4. Add your cooking oil to a pot and allow it to reach 370 degrees. Once oil is ready, add your Crab Cake Egg Rolls and cook them for 6 minutes or until golden brown. Avoid crowding the pot; you want these to cook evenly.

5. Once complete, remove from oil and place on a wire rack to drain off extra oil and to cool a bit before serving. Plate your Crab Cake Egg Rolls along with the sauce below and ENJOY!

HOMEMADE REMOULADE SAUCE

1. Into a medium mixing bowl, combine the following ingredients for the sauce: 2 tbsp Mayo of choice, 1 tbsp Ketchup, 1 tbsp Grey Poupon Dijon Mustard, 1 tsp Hot Sauce of choice, 1 tsp Garlic Powder, 1 tsp Onion Powder, 1 tbsp Fresh Lemon Juice, Black Pepper and Parsley.
2. Stir these ingredients well, and you have a very tasty Remoulade Sauce! ENJOY!

RED VELVET CHICKEN SANDWICH

 4 Servings   Recipe   🍲 30 Minutes

INGREDIENTS:

- (2) Boneless Chicken Breast
- 1.5 tbsp Unsweetened Cocoa Powder
- 2/3 cup Mustard
- 1/3 cup Honey
- 1/2 cup Buttermilk
- 1 cup Cornstarch
- 1 cup Vegetable Oil
- 1 cup Domino Golden Sugar
- 2.5 cups All-Purpose Flour
- 3 cups Peanut Cooking Oil
- 2 tbsp Red Food Coloring
- 1 tsp Baking Soda
- 1 tsp White Distilled Vinegar
- 1 tsp OSMO White Flakey Salt
- 2 tsp Pure Vanilla Extract
- 1 Egg

SEASONINGS:

- 3 tbsp Badia Black Garlic
- 3 tbsp Cajun Seasoning
- 3 tbsp Badia Poultry Seasoning
- 3 tbsp Dellalo's Rosemary & Garlic Seasoning
- 3 tbsp Delallo's Italian Herbs Seasoning

DIRECTIONS:

1. Remove the Chicken Breast from its package, cut them in half to make fillets, and clean the chicken in vinegar, water, and lemons. Once cleaned, pat dry and place in a large mixing bowl for seasoning.
2. Into the mixing bowl, add Mustard and Delallo's Rosemary & Garlic Seasoning, then thoroughly massage into Chicken fillets until well combined.
3. Into that same bowl, add All-Purpose Flour and Cornstarch. Place a lid on top and shake for 2-3 minutes until well coated.
4. In a 12-inch cast iron skillet, pour Peanut Cooking Oil and allow it to reach 350 degrees. Once the oil is ready, begin adding in Chicken fillets carefully.
5. Fry the Chicken fillets for 10-12 minutes or until the internal temperature reaches 165 degrees, then remove them from the oil and place them onto a wire rack to drain off the fat.

6. In a medium mixing bowl, combine dry ingredients; AP Flour, Domino Golden Sugar, Baking Soda, Himalayan Pink Salt, and Hershey's Unsweetened Cocoa Powder, then mix ingredients until well combined.
7. In another medium mixing bowl, combine wet ingredients, which consist of Vegetable Oil, Buttermilk, White Distilled Vinegar, Pure Vanilla Extract, Red Food Coloring, and 1 Egg, then mix ingredients until well combined.
8. Pour wet ingredients into the dry ingredients mixing bowl and fold in your cake mixture until both dry and wet mixtures have combined.
9. Grab your waffle maker, pour in your batter, and cook them for 1-2 minutes or until your waffle maker timer goes off.
10. Once your waffles have finished, remove them from the waffle maker and cut them into four pieces. These will be used as the bread for your sandwiches.
11. Place your Chicken Breast on one piece of a Red Velvet Waffle. Drizzle some honey on the Chicken Breast, then top it off with another Waffle and powdered sugar on top of the waffle! ENJOY!

CAJUN BUTTER LOBSTER TAILS

 4 Servings   Recipe   20 Minutes

INGREDIENTS:
- (4) Lobster Tails
- (4) Garlic Cloves, Minced
- (2) Stick KerryGold Garlic Herb Butter
- (1) Shallot, Minced
- (1) Lemon, Zest
- 1 cup Parmesan Cheese, Grated
- 1/4 cup Parsley Flakes
- 3 oz Sutter Home Pinot Grigio
- 3 tbsp Avocado Oil

SEASONINGS:
- 2 tsp Old Bay Garlic & Herb Seasoning
- 2 tsp Kingsford Lemon Pepper Seasoning
- 2 tsp Smoked Paprika
- 2 tsp Cajun Seasoning
- 1 tsp Crushed Red Pepper Flakes

DIRECTIONS:
1. Remove the Lobster Tails from the package, rinse them off under cool water, remove any grit that may be left behind, and place them on a cutting board.
2. Take a sharp Chef's Knife and split your lobster tails right down the middle. Rinse off any small shells left behind after cutting them.
3. Pat tails dry as possible for seasoning, then season your lobster tails with Old Bay Garlic & Herb Seasoning and Kingsford Lemon Pepper Seasoning, then massage into the Lobster Tails.
4. In a large skillet on medium heat, melt a half stick of Kerry Gold Garlic & Herb Butter.
5. Once melted, add the Lobster Tails shell side up and cook them for 3-5 minutes or until they reach an internal temperature of 145 degrees, then remove them from the skillet.

6. In the same skillet, pour in Avocado Oil with Minced Garlic and Shallots. Cook the veggies for 1-3 minutes, then run in Pinot Grigio. Allow the wine to reduce, then add Crushed Red Pepper Flakes, Cajun Seasoning, and another half stick of Kerry Gold Garlic & Herb Butter.
7. Once the butter has melted into the sauce, turn off the heat, then add the Lobster Tails back to the skillet with your Cajun Butter Sauce. Baste the Lobster Tails in the sauce.
8. Sprinkle about half a cup of Parmesan Cheese on top of the Lobster Tails and some fresh Parsley and Lemon Zest.
9. Grab a plate or eat straight out of the skillet and ENJOY!

GRILLED LEMON HONEY BUTTER LOBSTER TAILS

 2 Servings   Recipe   30 Minutes

INGREDIENTS:
- (4) Lobster Tails
- (2) Lemons
- 2 tbsp Parsley Flakes
- 3 tbsp Mike's Hot Honey
- 4 tbsp Olive Oil
- 4 tbsp Butter

SEASONINGS:
- 2 tsp Old Bay Lemon & Herb seasoning
- 4 tsp Old Bay Garlic & Herb seasoning
- 4 tsp Cajun seasoning

DIRECTIONS:
1. Preheat your indoor grill or outdoor grill to 400 degrees.
2. Rinse off Lobster Tails, removing any grit that may be left behind, then place on a cutting board.
3. Grab a pair of Shears and cut the tops of Lobster Tails to the tail end. Take a sharp Chef's Knife and split your lobster tails down the middle without completely cutting through the shell.
4. Rinse off any small shells left behind after cutting them. Pat tails as dry as possible for Oil and seasonings.
5. Pour some olive oil over the tails and season them with Old Bay garlic, herb seasoning, and Cajun seasoning, then thoroughly massage them into the tails.
6. Once seasoned, lay them on the grill, meat side with a couple of lemons, and cook the Tails for 3-5 minutes or until they reach an internal temp of 145 degrees.

7. Try not to move them while cooking to ensure excellent grill marks. Afterward, flip them to the shell side down, cut off the grill, and squeeze that fresh grilled lemon juice over the Tails.
8. Remove them from the grill and set them aside to prepare the Lemon Honey Butter Sauce.
9. In a small pot on low heat, melt 4 tbsp of Butter. Once melted, pour some Mike's Hot Honey, some of that grilled Lemon Juice, Parsley Flakes, Old Bay Lemon and herb seasoning, then mix.
10. Plate your Lobster Tails alongside a delicious green veggie, pour that sauce over the tails and ENJOY!

CRAB STUFFED LAMB CHOPS

 4 Servings   Recipe   40 Minutes

INGREDIENTS:

- 2 lbs Lamb Chops Rack
- 1 lb Jumbo Lump Crab Meat
- 2 Sticks KerryGold Garlic & Herb Butter
- 1 Block Cream Cheese
- 1/2 Sweet Onion, Sliced
- 1 cup Parmesan Cheese
- 2 cups Spinach
- 8 tbsp Avocado Oil

SEASONINGS:

- 3 tsp Old Bay Garlic & Herb Seasoning
- 4 tsp Kinder's Prime Steak Seasoning
- 4 tsp Spiceology Black Magic Cajun seasoning

DIRECTIONS:

1. Preheat oven to 350 degrees.
2. In a 10-inch skillet on medium heat, melt half a stick of Garlic & Herb Butter then add in sliced Onions along with Spinach. Season veggies with Badia Complete Seasoning.
3. Sautee veggies for 3-5 minutes just until Spinach cooks down then shut off the heat. Add the sauteed spinach and onions to a medium mixing bowl.
4. Next, add in Cream Cheese, Jumbo Lump Crab Meat, Parmesan Cheese and Old Bay Garlic & Herb Seasoning then mix until well combined.
5. Remove the rack of Lamb from its package, grab a sharp chef's knife, then cut then into 2 bones each. Pat them as dry as possible to ensure seasonings stick.
6. Take your chef's knife and cut a 1-2 inch slit to the tops of the Lamb, creating a pocket for crab stuffing later.

7. Pour about 4 tbsp of Avocado Oil then season the Lamb Chops with Kinder's Prime Steak Seasoning and Spiceology Black Magic Cajun seasoning then massage ingredients into the Lamb Chops thoroughly.

8. Once you have the Lamb Chops nice and seasoned add the crab stuffing to the slits of the lamb chops making sure they are packed in nice and tight. (If you have any Crab Stuffing left over, add in to a cast iron skillet, top it off with some Colby Jack Cheese and place in oven for 5-7 minutes for a crab dip option!)

9. Into a 12-inch skillet on high heat, pour in 4 tbsp of Avocado Oil, and once the oil is ready, add the Lamb Chops.

10. Depending on the size of your Lamb Chops, you want to sear for 2-4 minutes on one side, then flip and add 3 tbsp of Garlic & Herb Butter.

11. Once the butter melts, turn the heat off and baste the Lamb Chops in the butter then remove them from the skillet onto a wire rack.

12. Place the rack into preheated oven for 5-7 minutes to give the Lamb Chops a beautiful medium rare then remove from the oven.

13. Top them off with some more melted Garlic & Herb butter and enjoy with a side of homemade Garlic Mash Potatoes!

SHRIMP STIR FRY

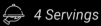 4 Servings   Recipe 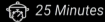 25 Minutes

INGREDIENTS:
- (15) Jumbo Raw Shrimp
- (1) Green Bell Pepper, Sliced
- (1) Red Bell Pepper, Sliced
- Fresh Green Beans, Chopped
- 2 tbsp Minced Garlic
- 3 tbsp Garlic & Herb Butter
- 1/2 lb Broccoli Florets
- 1/2 White Onion, Sliced
- 1/4 cup Green Onions, Sliced
- 1/4 cup Carrots, Shredded
- 1/2 cup Soy Sauce
- 1/4 cup Water
- 4 tbsp Toasted Sesame Oil
- 3 tbsp Avocado Oil
- 3 tbsp Oyster Sauce
- 3 tbsp Mirin
- 3 tbsp Golden Sugar
- 1 tbsp Brown Sugar
- 1.5 tsp Cornstarch

SEASONINGS:
- 2 tsp Roasted Garlic & Herb Seasoning
- 2 tsp Cajun Seasoning
- 2 tsp White Pepper
- 3 tsp Badia Complete Seasoning

DIRECTIONS:
1. Begin by rinsing the shrimp in cool water then deshell them. Afterward, pat them as dry as possible and place them in a medium mixing bowl.
2. Season the shrimp with Roasted Garlic & Herb Seasoning and Cajun Seasoning then mix until well combined.
3. In a large skillet on medium/high heat, pour in Avocado Oil along with the Shrimp. Cook the Shrimp for 2-4 minutes on each side.
4. After the first flip, add in 3 tbsp of Garlic & Herb Butter and allow it to melt. Once it melts, give the Shrimp a good toss then remove them from the skillet.
5. In a small mixing bowl, add in Soy Sauce, Oyster Sauce, Mirin, Brown Sugar, White Pepper, Cornstarch and Water then whisk together until well combined.

6. In a large Wok or Skillet on medium/high heat, pour in Sesame Oil along with some Minced Garlic then add the sliced White Onions along with the shredded Carrots.
7. Saute the Onions and Carrots for 2-3 minutes then add the Broccoli Florest along with the Sweet Peppers and Green Beans.
8. Season the veggies with Badia Complete Seasoning then saute them for another 3-5 minutes. (You don't want to cook the veggies too long. Still want a crunch to them.
9. Once the veggies are cooked to your liking, add the sauce to the pan along with the Shrimp. Give everything a nice mix until all the ingredients are well combined.
10. Cook for an additional 3-5 minutes so that the sauce can get thick and really incorporate with the shrimp and veggies.
11. Once you have the desired look and taste, grab a couple bowls, add some white rice to one side and the Shrimp and veggies on the other.
12. Top if off with some sesame seeds and green onion and ENJOY!

SALMON ALFREDO STUFFED BELL PEPPERS

 3 Servings   Recipe   60 Minutes

INGREDIENTS:
- 1.5 lb Salmon Filet
- (1) Box Fettuccine Noodles
- (6) Sweet Bell Peppers
- (5) Garlic Cloves, peeled
- 3 tbsp Minced Garlic
- 3 tbsp Minced Shallots
- 6 tbsp Garlic & Herb Butter
- 6 tbsp Avocado Oil
- 1.5 cups Broccoli Florets
- 1/2 cup Parmesan Cheese, Shredded
- 2 cups Heavy Cream
- 2 cups Broccoli Florets

SEASONINGS:
- 4 tsp Garlic & Herb Pepper Seasoning
- 4 tsp Smoked Paprika
- 3 tsp Badia Complete Seasoning
- 4 tbsp All-Purpose Seasoning
- 2 tsp Black Pepper

DIRECTIONS:
1. Preheat oven to 375 degrees.
2. Remove Salmon from the package, and lay it on a non-stick baking sheet. Pat dry, then pour 3 tbsp of Avocado Oil over the Salmon then season with Garlic Herb Pepper Seasoning and Smoked Paprika on both sides.
3. In a 12-inch skillet on medium/high heat, pour in 3 tbsp of Avocado Oil lay the Salmon in once the skillet is nice and hot. Sear the Salmon for 3-6 minutes on each side.
4. After you flip the Salmon for the first time, add 3 tbsp of Butter, and Garlic Cloves.
5. Once the butter has melted and infused with the garlic, base the Salmon with the butter. Once complete, remove the Salmon from the skillet, place it on a wire rack, pour the rest of that infused butter over the Salmon, then place the rack in the oven for 10-15 minutes or until the Salmon reaches an internal temperature of 145 degrees.
6. Bring 3 cups of water along with OSMO White Flakey Salt to a boil in a medium boiling pot. Once water is boiling, add one box of Fettuccine

Noodles, then reduce heat to medium and cook noodles for 11-12 minutes or until aldente.

7. Once the pasta is complete, turn off the heat, drain off the water, and sit aside to prepare veggies and alfredo sauce.

8. In a 10-inch skillet on medium heat, melt 3 tbsp of Butter. Once the butter has melted, add Minced Garlic and Minced Shallots, then, saute them for 1-2 minutes before adding in Broccoli Florets.

9. Add the Broccoli Florets after a couple minutes, season veggies with Badia Complete Seasoning then saute everything for 4-5 minutes before adding in Heavy Cream.

10. Next, reduce heat to medium/low heat and pour in Heavy Cream, All-Purpose Seasoning, Black Pepper, and Parmesan Cheese, then allow the sauce to come to a simmer.

11. Once it has started simmering, turn off the heat and check to see if it is the right consistency you like, then add Fettuccine Noodles to the skillet with the sauce.

12. Give your pasta a good toss in that sauce, then sit aside to prepare Bell Peppers. Cut the tops and gut the insides the Bell Peppers. Place the bell peppers in 8x10 baking dish then begin stuffing them with Cheese, then some Salmon, some Pasta Alfredo, more Salmon, and finally top it off with more cheese.

13. Add about half a cup of water to the bottom of the baking dish, then place in the oven for 15-20 minutes. Once complete, remove them from the oven, add a couple to a plate and ENJOY!

SEAFOOD GUMBO

 6 Servings　 Recipe　 2 Hours 30 Minutes

INGREDIENTS:

- 1.5 lbs Snow Crab Legs
- 1.5 lbs Jumbo Shrimp
- 1 lb Cajun Style Andouille Sausage
- 8 oz Jumbo Lump Crab Meat Fresh Parsley, Minced
- (1/2) White Onion, Diced
- (1) Green Pepper, Diced
- (2) Celery Stalks, Diced
- (4) Garlic Cloves, Minced
- (3) Bay Leaves
- 2 cups Chicken Broth
- 2 cups Seafood Stock
- 1 cup Cooking Oil
- 1 cup AP Flour
- 3 tbsp Olive Oil
- 1 tsp Better Than Bouillon Lobster Base

SEASONINGS:

- 3 tsp Garlic Powder
- 3 tsp Onion Powder
- 3 tsp Tony's Chacheres Creole
- 3 tsp Black Pepper
- 3 tsp Cajun Seasoning
- 3 tsp All-Purpose Seasoning
- 2 tsp Badia Complete Seasoning

DIRECTIONS:

1. Begin by getting a 12-inch skillet and turning the heat low. Once the skillet gets warm, pour in Cooking Oil along with the AP Flour.
2. The Roux is the most crucial step when making a good Gumbo, so low and slow will be the best option. Stir the Roux constantly to ensure it doesn't burn.
3. Keep stirring until the Roux has a Dark Chocolate color to it. Be mindful of getting to the desired color for the Roux; it can take 1-2 hours.
4. Once the Roux has gotten to your desired color, remove it from the heat and set it aside to prepare the rest of the recipe.
5. Next, slice the Cajun-style Andouille sausage into quarter-size shapes. Then, pour in Olive Oil along with the sliced Cajun Sausage in a large Dutch oven pot on medium heat.
6. Sauté the sausage for 3-5 minutes, long enough to get a nice char on them, then remove them from the skillet to prepare the veggies.

7. In that same skillet the sausage was prepared in, add the diced White Onion, Celery, Green Pepper, and minced Garlic. Season the veggies with some Badia Complete Seasoning, then mix until well combined.

8. Next, add the Roux to the veggies and some Seafood Stock, Chicken Broth, and Better Than Bouillon Lobster Base, then whisk the ingredients together thoroughly.

9. Season the Gumbo with Garlic Powder, Onion Powder, Black Pepper, All-Purpose Seasoning, Cajun Seasoning, and Tony's Chacheres Creole Season, then mix again.

10. Place a lid on the Gumbo, reduce the heat to Medium/Low to have a rolling simmer, then allow the Gumbo to stew for an hour while stirring occasionally so nothing sticks to the bottom of the pot.

11. When there are 15 minutes left for the Gumbo to be finished, add the Shrimp, Crab Legs, Crab Meat, and some chopped Parsley for color.

12. Give everything a good mix, then place the lid back on for 15 minutes to allow the seafood to cook. After the time has passed, give the Gumbo one more stir, then remove from the heat.

13. Serve this delicious Seafood Gumbo with White Rice and Garlic Bread! ENJOY!

BAKED TURKEY WINGS

 5 Servings   Recipe   1 Hour 20 Minutes

INGREDIENTS:

- 3 lb Turkey Wings
- 1/2 cups Olive Oil
- 1/2 cup Water
- 1/2 cup Tony Chacheres Injectable Butter
- 3 tbsp Worcestershire Sauce
- 2 tbsp Stir-In Garlic Paste 6 tbsp Avocado Oil
- 1 tsp Better Than Bouillon Roasted Chicken Base

SEASONINGS:

- 3 tsp Simply Spicy Spice All-Purpose Seasoning
- 3 tsp Simply Spicy Spice Garlic Herb Lemon Pepper Seasoning
- 2 tsp Smoked Paprika
- 2 tsp Black Pepper

DIRECTIONS:

1. Preheat oven to 375 degrees.
2. Rinse off Turkey Wings in cool water with fresh lemons and some vinegar if you have any. Remove any feathers on the wings, then pat dry for the next step.
3. Next, pour some Tony Chacheres Injectable Butter into a medium ramekin. Take the syringe with the Butter and inject each Wing with that delicious butter.
4. After you have injected the Wings with the Butter, place the Wings in a non-stick baking dish for seasoning.
5. Pour Avocado Oil over the Wings, then season them with Simply Spicy Spice All-Purpose Seasoning, Simply Spicy Spice Garlic Herb Lemon Pepper Seasoning, Smoked Paprika, and Black Pepper.
6. Massage in the seasoning with the Wings, ensuring they are evenly coated all over.

7. Next, add 1/2 cup of water to a measuring cup along with Worcestershire Sauce, Stir-In Garlic Paste, and Better Than Bouillon Roasted Chicken Base, then mix until well combined.

8. Pour this mixture into the bottom of the baking dish the Wings are in. DON'T completely submerge the wings in the sauce; just enough to cover the bottom of the baking dish.

9. COVER the baking dish with aluminum foil and place the dish in the oven for 1 hour. After the hour has passed, crank the heat up to 425 degrees, then REMOVE the foil.

10. Flip the Wings, then place them back in the oven for 10 minutes, then flip one and back in the oven for the final time for another 10 minutes to brown.

11. Once the Turkey Wings have finished, pull them out of the oven and serve with homemade Mac N'Cheese. Enjoy!

BROCCOLI & CHEDDAR POT PIE

 3-5 Servings   *Recipe*   *35 Minutes*

INGREDIENTS:

- 5 cups Vegetable Broth
- 2 cups Broccoli, chopped
- 1 cup Carrots, shredded
- 1 cup Heavy Whipping Cream
- 1 cup Cheddar Cheese, Shredded
- 2 tbsp Kerry Gold Garlic & Herb Butter
- 1 tbsp All-Purpose Flour
- 1 tsp Garlic Paste
- (1) Shallot, Diced
- (1) Pillsbury Crescent Dough Sheet
- (2) Eggs

SEASONINGS:

- 3 tbsp Salt Free All-Purpose Garlic & Herb Seasoning
- 2 tbsp Osmo White Flakey Salt

DIRECTIONS:

1. In a large boiling pot on medium heat, add Kerry Gold Garlic, herb butter, diced shallots, and garlic paste.
2. Sauté the shallots for a few minutes until they are translucent, then add in some- All-purpose flour and whisk ingredients together.
3. Next, pour Vegetable Broth with the chopped Broccoli and shredded Carrots.
4. Season the pot with Salt-Free All-Purpose Garlic and herb Seasoning and Osmo White Flakey Salt, then mix. Cover with a lid and bring to a boil.
5. Once it has begun boiling, remove the lid, pour in Heavy Whipping Cream and shredded Cheddar Cheese, then mix until well combined or until the cheese melts.
6. Cut the heat off and set aside to prepare Pillsbury Cresent Dough. Grab your preferred ramekin size and place it on the crescent dough. Trace out a circle using the bottom of the ramekin, and this will be the top for your Pot Pie.

7. Now that you have the tops for your pies add the Broccoli and cheddar soup to the ramekins and the cutout dough.

8. Whisk a couple of eggs together and brush the eggs over top of the dough. Place the ramekins in the oven for 8-10 minutes or until the tops are golden brown.

9. Remove the ramekins from the oven, give them a few minutes to cool, then dig in! ENJOY!

STEAK FOIL WRAPS

 3 Servings   Recipe   45 Minutes

INGREDIENTS:
- (2) New York Strip Steaks, Cubed
- (2) Russet Potatoes, Cut into Quarters
- (2) Sticks Kerry Gold Garlic & Herb Butter
- (1) Broccoli Head, Chopped
- (1) White Onion, Sliced
- (1) Block Cheddar Cheese, Shredded
- Fresh Parsley, Chopped
- 1 tsp Garlic Paste
- 3 tbsp Worcestershire Sauce

SEASONINGS:
- 2 tsp Kinder's Steak Blend
- 2 tsp Kinder's The Blend Seasoning
- 2 tsp Hidden Valley Ranch Seasoning

DIRECTIONS:
1. Preheat oven to 400 degrees.
2. Remove the Steaks from the pack, cut them into cubes, and place them in a medium size bowl.
3. Pour in Worcestershire Sauce, Garlic Paste, sliced White Onions, and Parsley, and season with a couple of teaspoons of Kinder's Steak. Blend the mix.
4. Next, cut the Russet Potatoes and Broccoli into quarters and place them into individual mixing bowls.
5. Melt one entire Kerry Gold Garlic & Herb Butter stick and pour half of the butter on the broccoli and the other half on the potatoes.
6. Season the broccoli and potatoes with Kinder's The Blend Seasoning and Hidden Valley Ranch Seasoning, and then mix.
7. Grab a couple of sheets of aluminum foil and add Steak, Potatoes, and Broccoli, then place a tablespoon of Kerry Gold Garlic and herb Butter on each one.

8. Wrap everything up and place it inside the oven for 30-40 minutes, depending on how you like your steak prepared.
9. Remove from oven, open it, and add the shredded cheddar to the potatoes or broccoli. Pull out your Torch if you have one, melt that cheese, and ENJOY!

BEEF SHORT RIBS

 3-5 Servings   *Recipe*   *3 Hours 15 Minutes*

INGREDIENTS:
- 6 Beef Short Ribs
- 1 White Onion, Chopped
- 4 Carrot Stalks, Chopped
- 4 Celery Stalks, Chopped
- 2 Bay Leaves
- 2 Fresh Rosemary Sprigs
- 2 Fresh Thyme Sprigs
- 2 Fresh Parsley Sprigs
- 1 Garlic Bulb
- 2 tbsp Avocado Oil
- 2 tbsp Butter
- 1 Bottle Snoop Dogg Cali Red Wine
- 3 cups Beef Broth
- 3 tbsp AP FLour
- 1 tbsp Tomato Paste

SEASONINGS:
- 1/2 cup Kinder's Prime Steak Seasoning
- 4 tsp Badia Complete Seasoning

DIRECTIONS:
1. Preheat oven to 325 degrees.
2. Remove Short Ribs from its package and pat dry as much blood as you can from the ribs, then season them generously covering all sides.
3. In a large dutch oven on medium/high heat pour in Avocado Oil, then begin searing the Short Ribs for 4-6 minutes on each side making sure you get a nice char.
4. Remove Short Ribs from the pot, reduce the heat to low and place them on a wire rack then set aside.
5. In the same pot the Short Ribs was prepared, add in chopped Onion, Carrots and Celery. Then season veggies with Badia Complete Seasoning then mix and cook for 4-6 minutes.
6. After cooking veggies down a bit, add in Butter and AP Flour then mix. Add in Tomato Paste then mix once more.
7. Next, pour in a full bottle Snoop Dogg Cali Red Wine then return the Short

Ribs back to the pot and pour in Beef Broth.

8. Finally, add in 2 Bay Leaves, 2 Fresh Rosemary Sprigs, 2 Fresh Thyme Sprigs, 2 Fresh Parsley Sprigs and 1 Garlic Bulb then cover and place in preheated oven.

9. Slow cook the Short Ribs for 3 hours minimum then once the 3 Hours have passed, remove them from the oven, remove the lid and enjoy that smell for a minute!

10. Carefully remove Short Ribs from the pot and sit them on a wire rack. Should be able to tell how tender they are by how easily you remove the bone!

11. Next, strain the pot that the ribs was prepared in leaving. only the sauce behind. Add this sauce to a skillet on medium heat then allow sauce to come to a simmer. Once it starts to simmer, remove from heat and now you have a nice sauce for Ribs.

12. In a plate or bowl full on mashed potatoes, place Short Ribs on top then drizzles sauce on top and garnish with fresh parsley. ENJOY!

BEEF SHORT RIB CORNBREAD BOWL

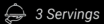 3 Servings   Recipe   2 Hours 45 Minutes

INGREDIENTS:
- (6) Beef Bone-In Short Ribs
- (1) Stella Rosa Il Conte Rosso, Bottle
- (2) Eggs
- (3) Carrots, Sliced
- (3) Celery Stalks, Sliced
- 1/2 White Onion, Sliced
- Fresh Thyme
- Fresh Rosemary
- Fresh Garlic
- Fresh Bay Leaves
- 1 tsp Baking Powder
- 2 tbsp Tomato Paste
- 4 tbsp Butter
- 4 tbsp Avocado Oil
- 1/4 cup Mike's Hot Honey
- 1 cup Yellow Cornmeal
- 1 cup Golden Sugar
- 1 cup Whole Milk
- 2 cups AP Flour
- 3 cups Beef Broth

SEASONINGS:
- 1 tsp OSMO White Flaky Salt
- 2 tsp Badia Complete Seasoning
- 3 tsp Kinders The Blend
- 6 tsp Spiceology Gaucho Steakhouse

DIRECTIONS:
1. Preheat oven to 350 degrees.
2. Remove the Short Ribs from the package, pat them dry, and place them in a mixing bowl. Season the ribs with Spiceology Gaucho Steakhouse Seasoning, then massage seasonings thoroughly.
3. In a large pot or Dutch oven on medium/high heat, pour in a couple of tablespoons of Avocado Oil. Once ready, add the Short Ribs to the pot and sear them on each side for 4-6 minutes.
4. Once finished, remove the Ribs from the pot and set them aside. In the same pot, reduce the heat to medium/low and add the veggies: sliced Carrots, Celery, and Onions.
5. Season the veggies with Badia Complete Seasoning, then saute them for 2-4 minutes. Add some Tomato Paste and a tablespoon of AP Flour, then mix until well combined.

6. Next, pour in beef broth with half a bottle of Stella Rosa Il Conte Rosso, fresh thyme, rosemary, and garlic, then return the short ribs to the pot.
7. Give the pot one final season with Kinders The Blend seasoning and cover the pot with an oven-safe lid. Place the pot in the oven for 2 hours and 30 minutes.
8. Once the time has passed, remove the pot from the oven, remove the lid, and watch how that bone slides right out! Set the Ribs aside to prepare the Homemade Cornbread.
9. Crank the temperature up on the oven to 400 degrees, then in a small mixing bowl, combine the following: Yellow Cornmeal, 1 cup of AP Flour, Baking Powder, Golden Sugar, OSMO White Flakey Salt, 2 Eggs, Mike's Hot Honey, and Whole Milk then mix.
10. Grab a small cast iron skillet and butter the bottom of the skillet with a couple of tablespoons of salted butter to help with the Cornbread not sticking after the cooking process.
11. Pour cornbread mix into the skillet, then place it in the oven for 15-20 minutes or until golden brown. And cooked all the way through.
12. Once complete, make a hole in the middle of the Cornbread with a ramekin and remove the middle. Add some creamy mashed potatoes to the middle, along with your Short Ribs and veggies.
13. Top it off with some of the sauce from the pot, and ENJOY!

BOURBON TERIYAKI STEAK BOWL

🍽 *4 Servings*   ✱ *Recipe*   🍲 *30 Minutes*

INGREDIENTS:
- (3) Thick Cut NY Strip Steaks, Sliced
- (5) Garlic Cloves, Minced
- (1) White Onion, Sliced
- 1.5 lbs Fresh Green Beans
- 2 tbsp Brown Sugar
- 3 tbsp Avocado Oil
- 2 cup Cornstarch
- 1/2 cup Soy Sauce, Less Sodium
- 1/4 cup Pineapple Juice
- 1.5 Shots of Bourbon, Uncle Nearest preferred

SEASONINGS:
- 4 tsp Spice King Grilled Steak & Burger Seasoning
- 3 tsp Badia Complete Seasoning

DIRECTIONS:
1. Remove Steaks from its package and pat dry. Cut the steak into sliced strips and put the steak into a mixing bowl. Season the Steak strips with Spice King Grilled Steak & Burger Seasoning and mix.
2. To the same bowl, add a cup of Cornstarch and a little more of Spice King Grilled Steak & Burger Seasoning, then close with a lid and shake until each piece of steak is coated in cornstarch evenly.
3. Next, preheat a large skillet on medium/high heat, and once ready, pour in Avocado Oil along with the Steak strips. You want to sear the steak for 2 minutes on each side to get a nice char on them.
4. Once they have finished searing, remove them from the skillet, reduce the heat to medium/low, and add in minced Garlic, less sodium Soy Sauce, a couple of shots of your favorite Bourbon, Pineapple Juice, Brown Sugar, and a Cornstarch slurry made with a teaspoon of Cornstarch and hot water.

5. Mix the ingredients and bring the sauce to a rolling simmer. As the sauce comes to a simmer, it will start getting thick. Once it has reached your desired thickness, return the Steak slices to the skillet along with the onions and green beans.

6. Give everything a good mix together, add about a 1/8 cup of water into the mix so the sauce doesn't get too thick, cover with a lid and simmer for 5-7 minutes. Just long enough to cook down the veggies.

7. After time has passed, shut off the heat, grab a couple of bowls filled with white rice, add the Bourbon Teriyaki Steak on top, garnish with Sesame Seeds, and ENJOY!

CREAMY LEMON SHRIMP BOWL

 3-4 Servings   *Recipe*   *30 Minutes*

INGREDIENTS:
- 2 lb Extra Large Shrimp
- 1 Box Fettuccini Noodles
- 2 tbsp Fresh Parsley, Chopped
- 2 tbsp Garlic Paste
- 3 tbsp Fresh Lemon Juice
- 3 tbsp Sutter Home Pinot Grigio Wine
- 4 tbsp Olive Oil
- 4 tbsp Butter, Salted
- 2 cups Heavy Cream
- 1/2 cup Parmesan Cheese, Grated

SEASONINGS:
- 3 tsp Kinder's Lemon Butter Garlic Seasoning
- 3 tsp Kingsford's Garlic & Herb Seasoning
- 3 tsp The Spice Lady GG's Frito Seasoning
- 2 tsp Smoked Paprika
- 2 tsp OSMO White Flakey Salt
- 2 tsp Black Pepper

DIRECTIONS:
1. Rinse off and peel your [large, raw, deveined] shrimp, then pat the shrimp dry, removing as much moisture as possible. Then, place the shrimp in a medium mixing bowl for seasoning.
2. Pour in a couple of tablespoons of Olive Oil, then season with Kinder's Lemon Butter Garlic seasoning, Smoked Paprika, and chopped Parsley. Mix until the shrimp is fully coated.
3. In a skillet on medium/high heat, pour in a tablespoon of Olive Oil and add the Shrimp. Cook the shrimp on each side for 3-4 minutes; add a couple of tablespoons of butter, remove the shrimp from the skillet, and set aside.
4. In the same skillet, melt a few more tablespoons of Butter. Once the butter has melted, add [1 tsp of Garlic Paste, 1 tbsp of fresh lemon juice, 3 tbsp of Sutter Home Pinot Grigio Wine, and 1/2 cup of Heavy Cream] in that order.
5. Bring the sauce to a light simmer, then season with The Spice Lady GG's Frito seasoning, Osmo White Flakey Salt, Black Pepper, and some grated Parmesan Cheese. Mix until well combined, then cut the heat.

6. Begin building your bowl with your choice of rice, a green veggie, and finally, that delicious shrimp you made earlier. Pour the sauce over your shrimp bowl, garnish with a little Parsley, and ENJOY!

CRAB & SALMON PASTA BREAD BOWL

 4 Servings   *Recipe*    *50 Minutes*

INGREDIENTS:
- (4) Skinless Salmon Fillets
- (8) oz Jumbo Lump Crab Meat
- (6) inch Loaf Artisan Bread
- 2 tbsp Minced Garlic
- 2 tbsp Minced Shallots
- 4 tbsp Butter, Salted
- 8 tbsp Avocado Oil
- 1/2 cup Grated Parmesan Cheese
- 2 cups Baby Spinach
- 2 cups Malfaldine Pasta
- 2 cups Heavy Cream
- 4 cups Water

SEASONINGS:
- 1 tsp Delallo's Roasted Garlic & Cheese Seasoning
- 2 tbsp Southern Made Creole Seasoning
- 2 tbsp OSMO White Flakey Salt
- 2 tbsp Black Pepper
- 2 tbsp Smoked Paprika
- 2 tbsp Kinder's Italian Chop House Seasoning
- 2 tbsp Lemon Herb Seasoning

DIRECTIONS:
1. Preheat oven to 400 degrees.
2. Remove the Salmon filets from the package, pat them dry, and lay them on a lined baking sheet with parchment paper for seasoning. Begin by drizzling about 4 tbsp of Avocado Oil on the Salmon, then season them with Lemon Herb Seasoning, Kinder's Italian Chop House Seasoning, and Smoked Paprika.
3. Massage the seasoning into the Salmon on both sides, then place the salmon in the preheated oven for 13-15 minutes or until it reaches an internal temperature of 145 degrees
4. Bring 4 quarts of water to a boil on high heat, then add about 3 tbsp of Salt to the water along with the Pasta. Reduce the heat to Medium and cook the pasta for 10-12 minutes UNCOVERED. Once the pasta is done, turn off the heat, drain the water from the pasta, and set aside.
5. In a 10-inch skillet on medium heat, drizzle in about 2 tbsp worth of Avocado Oil. Once the skillet is ready, add minced Garlic and Shallots. Saute them for 2-3 minutes, then add the Spinach.

6. Incorporate the garlic and shallots with the spinach, and then begin adding the Jumbo Lump Crab Meat and heavy cream. Next, mix the sauce with Southern Made Creole Seasoning, Black Pepper, grated Parmesan Cheese, and OSMO White Flakey Salt.

7. Allow the sauce to come to a rolling simmer. Once the heat has dropped to low, add the cooked pasta, then mix until all ingredients are well combined. Cut the heat and set aside.

8. In a small ramekin, melt half a stick of salted butter. Once melted, season it with Delallo's Roasted Garlic & Cheese Seasoning and mix. Next, cut the middle piece out of your 6-inch loaf of Artisan Bread, then begin brushing the garlic butter inside and outside the bread.

9. Place bread onto a wire rack baking sheet and straight into the oven for 4-5 minutes or until golden brown, then remove it from the oven to begin building the pasta bread bowl.

10. Now that the bread is fresh out of the oven, begin filling the inside of the bread bowl with pasta. Once it is filled, add the salmon fillets on top. Drizzle some of that delicious sauce over the salmon, then finish with a sprinkle of Parmesan Cheese and Parsley for color.

11. Place this masterpiece back into the oven for 2-4 minutes just to make sure everything is still nice and warm. Then remove it from the oven, cut off your desired piece, and ENJOY!

SALMON BURGER

 4 Servings   Recipe   45 Minutes

INGREDIENTS:
- 2 lbs Atlantic Salmon
- 16 oz Jumbo Lump Crab Meat
- 1 Box Penne Noodles
- 1 tsp Garlic Paste
- 2 tbsp Minced Shallots
- 2 tbsp Hot Sauce
- 3 tbsp Avocado Oil
- 3 tbsp Dijon Mustard
- 4 tbsp Kerry Gold Garlic & Herb Butter
- 1/4 cup RITZ Garlic Butter Crackers
- 1 cup Grated Parmesan Cheese
- 2 cups Heavy Cream
- 3 cups Water

SEASONINGS:
- 1 tsp Tony Chachere's Original Creole Seasoning
- 1 tsp Old Bay Garlic & Herb Seasoning
- 1 tsp Kinder's Cracked Lemon Pepper Seasoning
- 2 tsp Cajun Seasoning
- 3 tsp Simply Spice Garlic Herb Lemon Pepper Seasoning
- 3 tsp Smoked Paprika
- 4 tsp Black Pepper
- 4 tsp Parsley
- 6 tsp OSMO White Flakey Salt

DIRECTIONS:
1. Preheat oven to 400.
2. Remove Salmon from the package, pat dry any moisture left behind for seasonings, then cut out 3-4 fillets.
3. Once the Salmon is cut into fillets, slice a 2-inch slit in the middle of salmon pieces for the Crab stuffing for later.
4. Next, pour some Avocado Oil over Salmon fillets then season them with Simply Spice Garlic Herb Lemon Pepper seasoning, Smoked Paprika, and 3 tsp of Black Pepper.
5. Be sure to rub seasoning in thoroughly including in the slit where the crab stuffing will sit.
6. In a medium mixing bowl, add in Dijon Mustard, Hot Sauce, Old Bay Garlic & Herb seasoning, Kinder's Cracked Lemon Pepper seasoning, Tony Chachere's Original Creole Seasoning, Parsley, and RITZ Garlic Butter crackers then mix until well combined.
7. Next, add the Jumbo Lump Crab meat to mixture and fold in crab meat

DO NOT STIR. Once your crab mixture is ready, start stuffing your Salmon fillets.

8. Once the fillets stuffed, place the Salmon on a wire rack and put them into the oven to cook for 20-25 minutes or until the internal temparatue of the Salmon is at 145 degrees.

9. Remove your Crab Stuffed Salmon from the oven and sit aside to prepare pasta and the sauce.

10. Bring 3 cups of water along with OSMO White Flakey Salt to a boil in a medium boiling pot. Once water is boiling, add one box of Penne Noodles, then reduce heat to medium and cook noodles for 9-11 minutes or until aldente.

11. Once the pasta is complete, turn off the heat, drain off the water, and sit aside to prepare the sauce.

12. In a 12-inch skillet on medium heat, melt 4 tbsp of Kerry Gold Garlic & Herb Butter. Once the butter has melted, add in Minced Shallots and Garlic Paste. You want to saute them for 1-2 minutes before adding in the Heavy Cream.

13. Next, reduce heat to medium/low heat and pour in the Heavy Cream then seasoning the sauce with Cajun seasoning, 1 tsp Black Pepper, OSMO White Flakey Salt, Parsley and Grated Parmesan Cheese and mix.

14. Once the sauce has started simmering, check to see if it is the right consistency you like, cut off the heat and mix in the Penne Noodles with the sauce. Give your pasta a good toss in that sauce for 1-2 minutes to make sure all the ingredients are well combined.

15. Fill a couple bowls with your pasta along with one of the Crab Stuffed Salmon filets on top and ENJOY!

SLOW COOKED BBQ BEEF TIP SANDWICHES

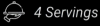 4 Servings   Recipe   2 Hours

INGREDIENTS:
- 2 lbs Chuck Roast
- 3 tsp White Distilled Vinegar
- 6 tbsp Butter (UNSALTED)
- 3 tbsp Olive Oil
- 3 tbsp Honey
- 1 cup Ketchup
- 1/4 cup Pineapple Juice
- 1/4 cup Mustard
- 1/4 cup W Sauce
- 2/3 cup Brown Sugar
- Dill Pickles (OPTIONAL)
- Ciabatta Rolls (OPTIONAL)
- French's Crispy Onion Straws (OPTIONAL)

SEASONINGS:
- 4 tsp BBQ Seasoning
- 4 tsp Spice King Grilled Steak & Burger seasoning
- 4 tsp Spice King Country BBQ Rub seasoning
- 2 tsp Chili Powder
- 2 tsp White Pepper
- 2 tsp Roasted Ground Cumin

DIRECTIONS:
1. Preheat oven to 350 degrees.
2. Remove Chuck Roast from the package, pat it dry, then cut the roast into 2-inch cubes and add them to a mixing bowl.
3. Pour about 4 tbsp of W Sauce, then season with Spice King Grilled Steak & Burger seasoning and Country BBQ Rub seasoning and thoroughly massage them into the pieces.
4. In a 10-inch cast iron skillet on high heat, pour in some Olive Oil along with the Chuck Roast cubes. Sear them on each side for 1-2 minutes to get that beautiful char color to them.
5. Remove the chuck cubes from the skillet and put them into a mixing bowl, then set them aside to prepare Homemade BBQ Sauce.
6. In the same cast iron on low heat, begin melting some Butter, and once melted, add in Ketchup, Mustard, 4 tbsp of W Sauce, White Distilled Vinegar, Honey, Pineapple Juice, Brown Sugar, Chili Powder, Cumin, BBQ seasoning then mix.

7. Allow your sauce to simmer, cut off the heat, and return the Chuck piece to the cast iron with the BBQ Sauce. Save some of the sauce for the toasted buns later.

8. Give the pieces a good toss in the sauce, then cover the cast iron with a lid and place the skillet into the oven for an 1 hour and 30 minutes

9. After time has passed, remove the skillet from the oven, remove the lid, and mix the pieces in that delicious Homemade BBQ Sauce. Next, it's time to assemble the sandwich!

10. Toast your choice of buns with a little Kerry Gold Garlic & Herb Butter; today, we used Ciabatta rolls by La Brea Bakery. Next, add your choice of toppings; I used a couple of slices of Dill Pickles and some Fried Onion Straws.

11. Finally, stack some delicious beef tips and provolone cheese onto the sandwich. Melt the cheese on top with a blow torch if you have it, or place it back in the oven for a few minutes to melt the cheese.

12. Once the cheese is melted, have these Slow Cooked BBQ Beef Tip Sandwiches with chips! Enjoy!

LAMB MAC N'CHEESE

 4 Servings   Recipe   40 Minutes

INGREDIENTS:
- (8) Lamb Loins or Chops
- 16 oz Box Barilla Cellentani Noodles
- 1.5 cups Whole Milk
- 1 Block Sharp Cheddar Cheese, Shredded
- 1 Block Mozzarella Cheese, Shredded
- 1 Block Colby Jack Cheese, Shredded
- 1 Stick Butter, Salted
- 4 tbsp AP Flour
- 4 tbsp W Sauce
- 4 tbsp Olive Oil

SEASONINGS:
- 2 tbsp Garlic Powder
- 2 tbsp Onion Powder
- 2 tbsp Black Pepper
- 2 tbsp Garlic & Herb seasoning
- 2 tbsp Smoked Paprika
- 4 tbsp Spice King Grilled Steak & Burger seasoning
- 4 tbsp Natures Promise Manhattan Steak Blend
- 6 tbsp OSMO White Flakey Salt
- 2 tsp Ground Mustard

DIRECTIONS:
1. Preheat oven to 350 degrees.
2. Remove the Lamb from the package and add them to a mixing bowl. Pour some W Sauce, then season with Spice King Grilled Steak & Burger seasoning and Nature's Promise Manhattan Steak Blend.
3. In a medium skillet on high heat, pour in Olive Oil and add the Lamb. Cook them for 2-3 minutes on each side for medium-cooked Lamb.
4. After the first flip, add a couple of tablespoons of butter, then base the lamb in the butter until it reaches your desired internal temperature and remove them from the skillet.
5. Bring 4 cups of water and 4 tbsp of OSMO White Flakey Salt to a boil, then add the Cellentani noodles once ready. Cook the noodles for 11 minutes, and once done, drain the water and set aside to prepare the cheese sauce.
6. In a medium saucepan on medium/low heat, melt 1 stick of Butter and once the Butter has melted, add in AP Flour along with Ground Mustard then whisk together until well combined.

7. Reduce the heat to low and whisk in the Whole Milk then begin adding in all 4 shredded cheeses; Sharp Cheddar, Mozzarella, Colby, and Monterey Jack Cheese.

8. Next, season the cheese sauce with Garlic Powder, Onion Powder, Black Pepper, Garlic & Herb seaoning and 2 tbsp of OSMO White Flakey Salt then stir until all the ingredients are well combined.

9. Begin adding the noodles to the cheese sauce and mix. Once you have the cheese and noodle combined, pour the Mac N' Cheese into a cast iron skillet.

10. Top off with more shredded cheese then place the dish into the oven for 30 minutes uncovered. Once complete, remove from the oven, add a couple Lamb Loins on top and ENJOY!

BAKED CRAB LEGS

 4 Servings   Recipe   15 Minutes

INGREDIENTS:
- 4 lbs Snow Crab Legs
- 1 Stick Unsalted Butter

SEASONINGS:
- 2 tbsp Tony Chachere's Supreme Crab Boil Seasoning
- 2 tbsp Cajun Seasoning
- 2 tbsp Lemon Pepper Seasoning

DIRECTIONS:
1. Preheat oven to 400 degrees.
2. Add the Crab Legs to a mixing bowl, then add some water. Take a vegetable cleaning brush and remove any black spots on them.
3. Drain off the water, then place the Crabs into a foil baking pan for seasoning. Season them with Tony Chachere's Supreme Crab Boil, Cajun seasoning, and Lemon Pepper seasoning.
4. Cut a whole stick of Unsalted Butter into tablespoons, place them on the legs, and spread them out.
5. Place the Crab Legs into the oven and cook them for 10-15 minutes. Once finished, remove them from the oven and baste the tops of the Crab Legs in that delicious butter at the bottom of the pan.
6. Make yourself a side of Broccoli, eat these Crab Legs straight out of the pan, and ENJOY!

STEAK FAJITAS

 3 Servings   Recipe   20 Minutes

INGREDIENTS:
- 1.5 lbs Skirt Steak
- (1) Red Bell Pepper, Sliced
- (1) Green Bell Pepper, Sliced
- (1) Yellow Bell Pepper, Sliced
- (1) White Onion, Sliced
- (4) Cloves Garlic, Minced
- 2 tbsp Parsley, Chopped
- 3 tbsp Worcestershire Sauce
- 4 tsp Fresh Lime Juice
- 1/2 cup Mozzarella Cheese, Shredded

SEASONINGS:
- 3 tsp Delallo's Rosemary Garlic Seasoning
- 3 tsp Kinders The Steak Blend Seasoning
- 3 tsp Tabitha Brown Very Good Garlic Seasoning

DIRECTIONS:
1. Remove the skirt steaks from the package and pat dry as much moisture as possible. Cut the steak into two-inch slices or strips, then place the steak in a mixing bowl for seasoning.
2. Next, Pour in Worcestershire Sauce and season with Kinders' The Steak Blend seasoning, Delallo's Rosemary Garlic seasoning, Parsley, and a couple of teaspoons of freshly squeezed Lime Juice. Mix.
3. In a 10-inch skillet on high heat, pour in a little Avocado Oil and the steak strips. The strips should generally cook fast, so it's best to cook them for 4-6 minutes. Once done, remove them from the skillet and set aside.
4. In the same skillet, reduce the heat to medium, melt a couple of tablespoons of butter, and add in sliced Red Pepper, Green Peppers, Yellow Pepper, White Onions, and minced Garlic.
5. Season the veggies with Tabitha Browns Very Good Garlic seasoning, then sauté them for 4-6 minutes before returning the steak slices to the skillet and mixing them together.

6. Reduce the heat to low, then sprinkle some freshly shredded Mozzarella Cheese all over the steak fajitas. Place a lid on the skillet for 2-4 minutes to allow the cheese to melt.
7. After the cheese has melted, turn off the heat, garnish with some freshly chopped parsley and a little more lime juice, and eat straight out of the skillet, fam! ENJOY!

HONEY LEMON BAKED CHICKEN

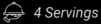 4 Servings   Recipe   1 Hour 15 Minutes

INGREDIENTS:
- (3) Chicken Leg Quarter
- (3) Whole Wings
- Fresh Rosemary
- Fresh Parsley
- 1 tsp Better Than Bouillon Roasted Chicken Base
- 3 tbsp Fresh Lemon Juice
- 4 tbsp Butter, Salted
- 1/4 cup Olive Oil
- 1/4 cup Honey
- 1 cups Chicken Broth

SEASONINGS:
- 4 tsp Rib Rack Chicken Seasoning
- 4 tsp Spice Theory Garlic Herb Pepper Blend
- 2 tsp Smoked Paprika

DIRECTIONS:
1. Preheat oven to 350 degrees.
2. Rinse the Chicken in cool water with fresh lemons and vinegar if you have any. Remove any feathers or yellow grit on the chicken, then pat it dry for the next step.
3. Next, pour a few tablespoons of Olive oil over the chicken and begin seasoning with Rib Rack Chicken Seasoning, Spice Theory Garlic Herb Pepper Blend, Smoked Paprika, and freshly chopped Parsley. Massage it thoroughly.
4. In a mixing bowl, combine the ingredients: honey, Chicken Broth, fresh Lemon Juice, and a teaspoon of Better Than Bouillon Roasted Chicken Base. Mix and set aside. This will serve as the Honey Lemon Sauce for later.
5. Heat a 12-inch cast iron skillet on medium/high heat. Add a couple of teaspoons of olive oil to the chicken. Sear the chicken for 6-8 minutes on each side.

6. Once seared, turn off the skillet's heat and add Rosemary, Butter, and the Honey Lemon Sauce from earlier. Be sure to pour the sauce along the outer rim of the skillet so that none of the seasonings come off the chicken.

7. Place the skillet in the oven and bake the chicken for an hour uncovered. Baste the chicken with the juices from the bottom of the skillet every 20 minutes to ensure even moisture throughout.

8. Once done, remove the skillet from the oven and admire that work of art in that skillet! Grab a bowl filled with your choice of rice, Lay a couple of pieces of chicken on top, pour some of that Honey Lemon sauce on top, and ENJOY!

SPICY TERIYAKI FRIED RIBS

 1-4 Servings　　 *Recipe*　　 *18 Minutes*

INGREDIENTS:
- 1.5 lbs Pork Ribs, Cut Individually
- (2) Eggs
- 1 tsp Cornstarch
- 1 tsp Water
- 2 tsp Fresh Lemon Juice
- 2 tsp White Sugar
- 3 tbsp Minced Garlic
- 3 tbsp Minced Ginger
- 3 tbsp Hot Sauce
- 4 tbsp Butter
- 5 tbsp Mustard
- 1/2 cup Soy Sauce
- 2 cup House Autry Medium Hot Seasoned Flour
- 3-4 cups Cooking Oil

SEASONINGS:
- 1 tsp Osmo White Flakey Salt
- 1 tsp Crushed Red Pepper Flakes
- 3 tsp Southern Made Creole Seasoning
- 3 tsp Kingsford Original AP Seasoning

DIRECTIONS:
1. Preheat 3-4 cups of cooking oil to 350-360 degrees.
2. Remove the ribs from the package, then pat dry. Next, remove the membrane from the back side of the ribs and begin cutting them into individual bones. Then, place the ribs in a mixing bowl.
3. Next, add Mustard, Hot Sauce of your choosing, and a couple of eggs, then season with Southern Made Creole seasoning and Kingsford Original AP seasoning and mix until well combined.
4. Into a separate mixing bowl, add your choice of seasoned flour or use AP flour and add the same seasonings you added to the ribs marinade, which should be fine.
5. Start adding the ribs to the flour and give them a good toss around, ensuring every inch of the ribs have been coated.
6. Once they have been coated, shake off any extra flour and add the ribs into the preheated cooking oil, only 3-5 bones at a time so that they all can cook evenly.

7. Fry the ribs for no longer than 6-8 minutes or until they reach an internal temperature of 145-150 degrees to ensure they stay nice and tender to eat!

8. After frying, remove them from the oil and put them onto a wire rack baking sheet to drain off any extra oil, then set aside to make the Spicy Teriyaki Sauce!

9. Into a small saucepan on medium/low heat, melt half a stick of butter, and once it melts, toss in some minced garlic and ginger. Saute the garlic and ginger for 1-2 minutes to release the flavors into the pan.

10. Next, pour in Soy Sauce, Worcestershire Sauce, fresh Lemon Juice, Sugar, Osmo White Flakey Salt, a cornstarch slurry that consists of cornstarch and a little water mixed, and Crushed Red Pepper flakes for the spicy effect.

11. Cut the heat to the sauce, then mix it well. Add the fried ribs to a mixing bowl, pour in that delicious sauce, give it a toss, sprinkle in some sesame seeds, then parsley for color, and ENJOY!

CAJUN BUTTER CHICKEN THIGHS

 3-4 Servings   *Recipe*   *1 Hour 15 Minutes*

INGREDIENTS:
- (8) Chicken Thighs
- Fresh Thyme
- Fresh Parsley
- 1 tbsp Better Than Bouillon Roasted Chicken Base
- 4 tbsp Butter, Salted
- 1/4 cup Olive Oil
- 1.5 cups Chicken Broth

SEASONINGS:
- 3 tsp Spiceology Cajun Seasoning
- 3 tsp Kinder's Italian Chop House Seasoning
- 3 tsp Granulated Chicken Bouillon

DIRECTIONS:
1. Preheat oven to 350 degrees.
2. Rinse the chicken thighs in cool water with fresh lemons and vinegar if you have any. This helps to remove any impurities. Remove any feathers or yellow grit on the chicken, then pat them dry. This step is important as it helps the seasonings adhere better to the chicken.
3. Next, pour a few tablespoons of olive oil over the chicken thighs and begin seasoning with Spiceology Cajun Seasoning, Kinder's Italian Chop House Seasoning, Chicken Bouillon, and freshly chopped Parsley. Massage the ingredients thoroughly on both sides of the thighs. This helps to distribute the flavors evenly.
4. Heat a 12-inch cast iron skillet on medium/high heat until it's just right, ready to sear the chicken to perfection. Add a couple of teaspoons of olive oil to the skillet, letting it shimmer and coat the surface. Carefully place the seasoned chicken in the skillet and let it sizzle on each side for 6-8 minutes, creating a beautiful golden crust.

5. Once they have finished searing, remove them from the skillet, reduce the heat to low, and pour in Chicken Broth with a tablespoon of Better Than Bouillon Roasted Chicken Base. Mix.

6. Return the Chicken Thighs to the skillet, then add Butter and Thyme. Place the skillet in the oven and bake uncovered for 45-50 minutes. Baste the chicken with the juices from the bottom of the skillet every 20 minutes to ensure even moisture throughout the chicken.

7. Once done, remove the skillet from the oven and admire its smell! Grab a bowl, add a Baked Potato, Southern-style kale Greens, and a couple of juicy Chicken Thighs with that sauce drizzled over the top, and ENJOY!

GARLIC BUTTER STEAK & POTATO SKILLET

 4 Servings   *Recipe*   *35 Minutes*

INGREDIENTS:
- (2) Ribeye Steaks, Cubed
- (8) Baby Gold Potatoes, Quarter Cut into Wedges
- (5) Garlic Cloves, Minced
- (1) White Onion, Sliced
- (1) Broccoli Head, Chopped
- Fresh Parsley, Chopped
- 6 tbsp Butter, Salted
- 4 tbsp Avocado Oil

SEASONINGS:
- 2 tsp Kinder's Cracked Pepper Parmesan Seasoning
- 3 tsp Kinder's Italian Chop House Seasoning
- 3 tsp Weber Roasted Garlic & Herb Seasoning

DIRECTIONS:
1. Remove Steaks from its package and pat dry as much moisture as possible to ensure seasonings stick. Cut your steak into cubes and place it in a medium-sized mixing bowl.
2. Begin seasoning the steak with Weber Roasted Garlic & Herb seasoning, then massage into the steak.
3. Into a large skillet on medium/high heat, pour two tablespoons of Avocado Oil and seasoned Steak bites. Cook the Steak for 3-5 minutes on each side or until brown.
4. Once steak bites have finished, reduce heat to medium/low and add three tablespoons of butter, minced garlic, and freshly chopped parsley, then mix until well combined. Remove the steak from the skillet and put it into a mixing bowl, then set aside.
5. In that same skillet on medium heat, add chopped broccoli and two tablespoons of Avocado Oil, then season them with Kinder's Cracked Pepper Parmesan seasoning. Saute the broccoli for 5-7 minutes, remove them from the skillet, put them into a bowl, and set aside.

6. Finally, just as before, using the same skillet on medium/high heat, melt three tablespoons of Butter. Once melted, add the potatoes and season them with Kinder's Italian Chop House seasoning and mix.
7. Begin to give the Potatoes a nice sear on the inside parts of the potato for 2-3 minutes on each side. After searing them a bit, reduce the heat to low, pour in about a fourth cup of Water, and cover with a lid.
8. Once the water has evaporated from the skillet, give them a toss, check to see if they are fork tender, and if not, pour in a little more water and cover until they are done.
9. Return the heat to medium and toss in chopped white onions with the potatoes. Allow the onions to become translucent, which should take 3 minutes on medium heat.
10. Afterwards, add the Broccoli and Steak bites into the skillet with the potatoes and onions. Give all the ingredients a good mix, then finish with a sprinkle of fresh Parsley.
11. Grab a bowl or eat straight out of the skillet with this one gang! ENJOY!

NANNA'S BAKED MEATLOAF

 4 Servings   Recipe   45 Minutes

INGREDIENTS:

- 1 lb 80/20 Ground Beef
- 1/2 lb Ground Beef Sausage
- Fresh Parsley
- Fresh Parmesan Cheese, Grated
- Fresh Garlic, Minced
- (1/2) Yellow Onion, Diced
- (8) Garlic Butter Ritz Crackers, Crumbled
- (2) Eggs
- 5 tbsp Ketchup
- 4 tbsp Sweet Baby Rays BBQ Sauce
- 2 tbsp Mustard
- 2 tbsp Worcestershire Sauce
- Lipton Beefy Onion Soup Mix, 1 Pack

SEASONINGS:

- 1 tsp Kinder's Italian Chop House
- 1 tsp Spice Theory Garlic Herb Pepper Blend
- 1 tsp PS Smoky Texas BBQ Rodeo Rub
- 1 tsp Oregano
- 1 tsp Black Pepper

DIRECTIONS:

1. Preheat oven to 375 degrees.
2. Add the ground beef and sausage to a medium mixing bowl, then add all the wet ingredients: three tablespoons of Ketchup, a tablespoon of Worcestershire Sauce, a couple of Eggs, and Mustard.
3. Next will be the dry ingredients that will also include the seasonings, Kinder's Italian Chop House seasoning, Spice Theory Garlic Herb Pepper Blend, Oregano, Black Pepper, a pack of Lipton Beefy Onion Soup Mix, and crumbled Garlic Butter Ritz crackers then mix.
4. Finally, add veggies and aromatics to the mixing bowl, which includes some minced Garlic, diced Yellow Onions, freshly grated Parmesan Cheese, and fresh Parsley.
5. Mix once more until all the ingredients have been combined thoroughly.
6. Place the meat mixture on a lined baking sheet or a loaf pan if you have one, then form the meat mix into a loaf shape. Place the baking sheet tray or loaf pan into the oven to cook for 40 minutes. While the meatloaf

is cooking, grab a small ramekin to prepare the sauce to go on top of the meatloaf.

7. In a small ramekin, pour Sweet Baby Rays BBQ Sauce, two tablespoons of Ketchup, a tablespoon of Worcestershire Sauce, and a teaspoon of PS Smoky Texas BBQ Rodeo Rub, then mix.

8. After the 40 minutes have passed on the meatloaf, remove it from the oven, brush the sauce all over the meatloaf, then place it back in the oven for 5 minutes so that the sauce can stick to the meatloaf giving it a nice glaze on top.

9. Once the 5 minutes are up, remove it from the oven, cut the loaf into size slices for you and the family, and enjoy this with your favorite sides!

ONE-PAN CHICKEN & RICE

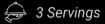 3 Servings   Recipe   50 Minutes

INGREDIENTS:
- (5) Chicken Legs
- (5) Garlic Cloves, Minced
- (1) Yellow Onion, Chopped
- (1) Red Bell Pepper, Chopped
- (1) Green Bell Pepper, Chopped
- (1) Broccoli Head, Chopped
- (1) Box Herb Butter Rice A Roni
- 3 tbsp Butter
- 1 cup Olive Oil
- 2.5 cups Chicken Stock or Water

SEASONINGS:
- 2 tsp Rib Rack Chicken Seasoning
- 2 tsp Badia Sazon Tropical Seasoning
- 2 tsp Dried tarragon
- 3 tbsp Chicken Bouillon

DIRECTIONS:
1. Welcome to our flavorful Chicken and Rice dish recipe! Let's start by preheating the oven to 350 degrees. Remove the Chicken Legs from the package, clean the legs with lemons and water, pat dry, and place into a mixing bowl for seasoning.
2. Now, let's season the Chicken Legs. Start by pouring about five tablespoons of olive oil over the legs. Then, sprinkle them with rib rack chicken seasoning, Badia Sazon tropical seasoning, and tarragon. Massage the oil and seasonings into the Legs thoroughly, then prepare the skillet. Pour a couple of tablespoons of Olive Oil into a cast iron skillet on medium/high heat. Once the oil is ready, sear chicken legs on each side for 7-9 minutes, remove them from the skillet, and place them aside.
3. Reduce the heat to medium and melt a couple of tablespoons of Butter in the same skillet. Once melted, add minced Garlic, chopped Onions, and Red and Green Bell Peppers.

4. Saute the veggies for 3-5 minutes before adding the Rice and Roni. Remove the seasoning pack from the box, then pour the rice into the skillet with the veggies.

5. Mix the veggies and rice, then pour in Chicken Broth or Water along with the chopped broccoli and Chicken Bouillon seasoning. Be sure to space everything excellently, even in the skillet, because now it's time to return the chicken legs to the skillet.

6. Cover the skillet with a lid and place it into the oven to bake for 35-40 minutes. After the time has passed, remove the lid from the skillet and place it back in the oven for 5 minutes to brown the top.

7. Once ready, remove the skillet from the oven, fluff the rice with a fork, and either eat from the skillet or grab some plates for the family and ENJOY!

SHORT RIB MINI TACOS

 6-8 Servings   *Recipe*   *2 Hours 10 Minutes*

INGREDIENTS:
- (5) Beef Bone-In Short Ribs
- (1) Stella Rosa Black Cherry
- (1) Pack Lipton Beefy Onion Soup Mix
- (6) Mission Sweet Hawaiian Soft Flour Street Taco Shells
- (3) Celery Stalks, Sliced
- Fresh Thyme
- Fresh Garlic, Minced
- 1/2 White Onion, Sliced
- 1 tbsp Better Than Bouillon Italian Herb Base
- 6 tbsp Avocado Oil
- 1 cup Mozzarella Cheese, Shredded
- 3 cups Beef Broth

SEASONINGS:
- 3 tsp Osmo Pinot Noir Salt
- 3 tsp Nick's Zesty Steak Seasoning
- 2 tsp Osmo White Flakey Salt
- 2 tsp Badia Complete Seasoning

DIRECTIONS:
1. Preheat oven to 375 degrees.
2. Remove the Short Ribs from the package, pat them dry, and place them in a mixing bowl. Season the ribs with Osmo Pinot Noir Salt and Nick's Zesty Steak seasoning, then massage the seasonings thoroughly.
3. In a large pot or Dutch oven on medium/high heat, pour in a couple of tablespoons of Avocado Oil. Once ready, add the Short Ribs to the pot and sear them on each side for 4-6 minutes.
4. Once finished, remove the Ribs from the pot and set them aside. In the same pot, reduce the heat to medium/low and add the veggies: minced Garlic, sliced Celery, and Onions.
5. Season the veggies with Badia Complete Seasoning and saute them for 2-4 minutes. Next, pour beef broth with half a bottle of Stella Rosa Black Cherry and fresh thyme.
6. Give the pot one final season with Osmo White Flakey Salt, a pack of Lipton Beefy Onion Soup Mix, and a tablespoon of Better than Bouillon Italian Herb Base. Mix everything well, then return the short ribs to the pot.

7. Cover the pot with an oven-safe lid and place it in the oven for 2 hours. Once the time has passed, remove the pot from the oven, remove the lid, pick up one of the ribs, and watch how that bone slides right out!

8. Take the ribs out of the pot and onto a cutting board. If you like to shred them, you can also do that. Cut the ribs down to bite-size cubes for the tacos, then place them in a bowl and set aside.

9. In a 12-inch skillet on medium heat, dip 2 - 3 Tortillas in the sauce from the ribs then straight into the skillet. Next, add the shredded Mozzarella Cheese, the shredded or cubed rib to one side of the tortillas, your choice of toppings, sauce from the pot the ribs were cooking in, more cheese, and fold the side into close the tacos.

10. Flip the tacos to seal the other side, remove them from the skillet, and straight onto the plate! Repeat these steps for more tacos. Grab a medium ramekin and dip the tacos in the sauce from the pot the ribs were cooking in. ENJOY!

FRIED CATFISH

 4 Servings   Recipe   30 Minutes

INGREDIENTS:
- 1.5 lb. Catfish
- (1) pack Louisiana Cajun Fish Fry
- (1) Egg
- 4 tbsp. Mustard
- 3 tbsp. Hot Sauce
- 3 cups Peanut Oil

SEASONINGS:
- 2 tsp. Kinders Lemon Butter Garlic Seasoning
- 2 tsp. Southern Made Creole Seasoning

DIRECTIONS:
1. Rinse off the Catfish in cool water, then pat dry. Lay out your fish on a cutting board, and depending on the size of the Catfish, you may need to cut it into long slices if the butcher shop still needs to slice the Catfish for you.
2. Once sliced to your desire, place the Catfish into a medium mixing bowl for seasoning. Next, pour mustard, hot sauce, one egg, and Kinder's lemon butter garlic seasoning. Southern-made Creole seasoning, then mix until well combined.
3. Pour a pack of Louisiana Cajun Fish Fry and the Catfish into a large mixing bowl. Place a lid on the bowl and give it a nice shake for about a minute or two, then remove the lid and check to see if all the Catfish is coated evenly.
4. In a 12-inch cast iron skillet on medium/high heat, pour in your choice of cooking oil; in this case, I used Peanut Oil. Once the cooking oil reaches 350-365 degrees, it is time to add in the Catfish.

5. Cook the Catfish for 12-15 minutes, flipping halfway through the cooking process to get the golden brown look to them. Once the Catfish has reached an internal temperature of 145-155 degrees, it is time to remove it from the skillet. (My family enjoys our fish cooked harder, so we do an additional 5-7 minutes in the cooking oil before removing it.)
6. Place them on a wire rack to drain extra oil from the grease. This helps to keep the catfish crispy and prevents it from becoming soggy. Then, grab a plate with your favorite side dish followed by your golden Catfish and ENJOY!

SPAGHETTI & MEATBALLS

 5 Servings   *Recipe*   *1 Hour*

INGREDIENTS:
- (2) lbs. Ground Beef
- (1) 12 oz. can Cento Crushed Tomatoes
- (1) Box Spaghetti Noodles
- (1) Eggs
- 1 cup freshly grated Parmesan Cheese
- 1 tbsp. Better Than Bouillon Italian Herb Base
- 4 tbsp. Olive Oil
- 2 tbsp. Sugar
- 3 tbsp. Minced Shallots
- 6 tbsp. Minced Garlic
- 6 tbsp. Parsley, Freshly Chopped
- 1/2 cup Garlic Butter Ritz Crackers, Crushed
- 3.5 cups Water

SEASONINGS:
- 3 tbsp. Delallo's Garlic & Tomato Seasoning
- 3 tbsp. Kinder's Italian Chop House Seasoning
- 2 tbsp. Osmo White Flakey Salt
- 1 tbsp. Badia Complete Seasoning
- 1 tbsp. Black Pepper

DIRECTIONS:
1. In a large mixing bowl, add in the [lean] Ground Beef along with an Egg, three tablespoons of minced Garlic, Kinder's Italian Chop House Seasoning, Better Than Bouillon Italian Herb Base, crushed Garlic Butter, Ritz Crackers, a couple tablespoons of freshly chopped Parsley, freshly grated Parmesan Cheese, and three tablespoons of Olive Oil then mix. Take a tablespoon of your meat mixture into your hand and roll until you make a golf ball-sized Meatball; place the Meatball onto a baking sheet, then repeat the same steps until you run out of the mixture.
2. Into a 12-inch skillet on medium/high heat, pour in two tablespoons of Olive Oil, and once the skillet is ready, add your Meatballs. Sear the Meatballs for 8-10 minutes, flipping every few minutes to ensure a good side sear.
3. Once you have seared your meatballs, remove them from the skillet and place them back onto the baking sheet or into a bowl, then set aside to make the spaghetti sauce.

4. In the same skillet, we prepare the Meatballs, reduce the heat on the skillet to medium, then add in minced Shallots, three tablespoons of minced Garlic, and Badia Complete seasoning.

5. Mix and saute the Garlic and Shallots for 2-3 minutes, then begin to pour in the can of Cento Crushed Tomatoes, half cup of water, Sugar, Osmo White Flakey Salt, Black Pepper, Delallo's Garlic & Tomato Seasoning, and a couple tablespoons of freshly chopped Parsley then mix until well combined.

6. Bring the sauce to a simmer, and then add the meatballs. Once you have them all in the skillet, cover it with a lid and allow the meatballs to stew in the sauce for 30 minutes on medium/low heat.

7. While the meatballs stew in the sauce, in a medium pot, bring 3 cups of water and a couple of teaspoons of Salt to a boil. When the water is boiling, add one box of [spaghetti] Noodles, then reduce the heat to medium and cook the noodles for 10-12 minutes. When done, drain off the water and set aside. After the meatballs have been stewing in the spaghetti sauce for 30 minutes, they should be cooked all the way through and still very juicy. Mix and taste the sauce to see if it's your liking, then grab a couple of bowls and dig in! ENJOY!

ONE-POT LASAGNA

 5 Servings   Recipe   35 Minutes

INGREDIENTS:
- (2) lbs. Ground Beef
- (1) lb. Ground Hot Italian Sausage
- (1) 24 oz. Rao's Homemade Marinara Sauce
- (1) Yellow Onion, Chopped
- 1 tbsp. Better Than Bouillon Italian Herb Base
- 1 tbsp. Olive Oil
- 2 tbsp. Tomato Paste
- 4 tbsp. Minced Garlic
- 4 tbsp. Basil, Freshly Chopped
- 1/2 cup Mozzarella Cheese, Shredded
- 1/2 cup Parmesan Cheese, Grated
- 1/2 cup Heavy Cream
- 2 cups Spinach
- 4 cups Chicken Broth

SEASONINGS:
- 3 tbsp. Delallo's Garlic & Tomato Seasoning
- 3 tbsp. Sun of Italy Ita;ian Spice Mix
- 2 tbsp. Osmo White Flakey Salt
- 1 tbsp. Badia Complete Seasoning

DIRECTIONS:
1. In a 4-6 quart pot on medium heat, saute some minced garlic, onions, and a little Badia Complete seasoning. Saute the veggies briefly, then add the ground hot Italian sausage and beef to the pot.
2. Cook down the meat until it is brown, then toss in some Spinach and cook that down into the meat mixture. Next, add Tomato Paste and Better Than Bouillon Italian Base, and then mix everything well.
3. Once stirred, add Chicken Broth, Rao's Homemade Marinara sauce, and Heavy Cream, then stir the pot again. Next, add some shredded mozzarella cheese and freshly grated Parmesan cheese.
4. Season the pot with Sun of Italy Spice Mix, Osmo White Flakey Salt, Delallo Garlic & Tomato seasoning, and freshly chopped Basil, then mix until well combined.
5. Finally, let the sauce come to a rolling simmer, then break up some Lasagna pasta and add it to the pot. Cover the pot with a lid and cook for

25-30 minutes or until the pasta is al dente, creating a deliciously rich and flavorful One-Pot Lasagna. Once complete, turn off the heat, give your One-Pot Lasagna a final stir, and admire that pot of deliciousness. Grab a couple of bowls for you and the family, and dig in! ENJOY!

PARMESAN CRUSTED SALMON

 5 Servings   Recipe   20 Minutes

INGREDIENTS:
- 1.5 lbs. Atlantic Salmon
- 2 tsp. Lemon Zest
- 2 tbsp. Lemon Juice
- 2 tbsp. Minced Garlic
- 4 tbsp. Fresh Parsley, Chopped
- 4 tbsp. Olive Oil
- 6 tbsp. Butter, Melted
- 1/2 cup. Italian Panko Breadcrumbs
- 1.5 cups. Parmesan Cheese, Grated

SEASONINGS:
- 2 tsp. Kinder's Italian Chop House Seasoning
- 2 tsp. Kingsford Lemon Pepper
- 2 tsp. Kinder's Cracked Pepper Parmesan Seasoning
- 2 tsp. Smoked Paprika

DIRECTIONS:
1. Preheat the air fryer to 400 degrees.
2. Remove Salmon from package and pat dry as much moisture as possible for seasoning.
3. Place the Salmon in a large oven safe dish lined with parchment paper on the bottom.
4. Drizzle some Olive Oil onto the Salmon then season the salmon with Kingsford Lemon Pepper, Kinder's Cracked Pepper Parmesan seasoning, and Smoked Paprika.
5. Massage the seasoning into the Salmon throughly ensuring it is fully coated the place the baking dish into the air fryer for 12 minutes.
6. While the Salmon is cooking, in a small mixing bowl add in Italian Panko Breadcrumbs, melted Butter, half a cup of freshly grated Parmesan Cheese, minced Garlic, Lemon Zest, Lemon Juice, and Kinder's Italian Chop House seasoning then mix until well combined.

7. After the time is up on the Salmon, remove it from the oven, freshly grate more Parmesan on top of the Salmon then begin adding the crusted parmesan mixture to the top of the Salmon.

8. Place the Salmon back into the air fryer for another 5 minutes to brown the top of the crust and once it is complete, remove it from the air fryer, cut out a couple fillets for you and the family, and pair it with your favorite sides. ENJOY!

SALISBURY STEAK

 4 Servings   Recipe   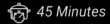 45 Minutes

INGREDIENTS:
- 1 lb 80/20 Ground Beef
- 1/2 lb Ground Beef Sausage
- Fresh Parsley
- Fresh Parmesan Cheese, Grated
- Fresh Garlic, Minced
- (1/2) Yellow Onion, Diced
- (8) Garlic Butter Ritz Crackers, Crumbled
- (2) Eggs
- 5 tbsp Ketchup
- 4 tbsp Sweet Baby Rays BBQ Sauce
- 2 tbsp Mustard
- 2 tbsp Worcestershire Sauce
- Lipton Beefy Onion Soup Mix, 1 Pack

SEASONINGS:
- 1 tsp Kinder's Italian Chop House
- 1 tsp Spice Theory Garlic Herb Pepper Blend
- 1 tsp PS Smoky Texas BBQ Rodeo Rub
- 1 tsp Oregano
- 1 tsp Black Pepper

DIRECTIONS:
1. Preheat oven to 375 degrees.
2. Add the ground beef and sausage to a medium mixing bowl, then add all the wet ingredients: three tablespoons of Ketchup, a tablespoon of Worcestershire Sauce, a couple of Eggs, and Mustard.
3. Next will be the dry ingredients that will also include the seasonings, Kinder's Italian Chop House seasoning, Spice Theory Garlic Herb Pepper Blend, Oregano, Black Pepper, a pack of Lipton Beefy Onion Soup Mix, and crumbled Garlic Butter Ritz crackers then mix.
4. Finally, add veggies and aromatics to the mixing bowl, which includes some minced Garlic, diced Yellow Onions, freshly grated Parmesan Cheese, and fresh Parsley.
5. Mix once more until all the ingredients have been combined thoroughly.
6. Place the meat mixture on a lined baking sheet or a loaf pan if you have one, then form the meat mix into a loaf shape. Place the baking sheet tray or loaf pan into the oven to cook for 40 minutes. While the meatloaf

is cooking, grab a small ramekin to prepare the sauce to go on top of the meatloaf.

7. In a small ramekin, pour Sweet Baby Rays BBQ Sauce, two tablespoons of Ketchup, a tablespoon of Worcestershire Sauce, and a teaspoon of PS Smoky Texas BBQ Rodeo Rub, then mix.

8. After the 40 minutes have passed on the meatloaf, remove it from the oven, brush the sauce all over the meatloaf, then place it back in the oven for 5 minutes so that the sauce can stick to the meatloaf giving it a nice glaze on top.

9. Once the 5 minutes are up, remove it from the oven, cut the loaf into size slices for you and the family, and enjoy this with your favorite sides!

CRISPY AIR-FRIED CHICKEN THIGHS

 3 Servings   *Recipe*   *40 Minutes*

INGREDIENTS:
- 3.5 lbs. Chicken Thigh
- 4 tbsp. Olive Oil
- 1/2 cup. Lefty's Spices Fish & Chicken Seasoned Flour Mix

SEASONINGS:
- 2 tsp. Spiceology Cajun Seasoning
- 2 tsp. Chicken Seasoning
- 2 tsp. Italian seasoning

DIRECTIONS:
1. Remove the Chicken Thighs from the package, rinse them in cool water and lemon juice, and pat them dry.
2. Next, place the Thighs in a bowl and pour in olive oil. Then season them with chicken seasoning, spiceology Cajun seasoning, Italian seasoning, and a half cup of Lefty's Spices seasoned flour mix.
3. Massage the ingredients into the thighs thoroughly, ensuring the thighs are evenly coated.
4. Place the Thighs on a foil-lined baking sheet, then put them into the air fryer at 360 degrees for 40 minutes. Flip the Thighs every 10 minutes to ensure an even crisp all over.
5. Once they are complete, remove the Thighs from Air Fryer and these Crispy and Healthy Fried Chicken Thighs with your favorite side dish and ENJOY!

ROASTED PERUVIAN CHICKEN

 6 Servings   *Recipe*   *1 Hour 20 Minutes*

INGREDIENTS:
- (1) Whole Chicken
- (1) Jalapeno
- (2) Green Onion Stalks, Chopped
- (2) Fresh Rosemary Spriggs
- (2) Cilantro Bunches
- (3) Whole Garlic Cloves
- 2 tbsp. Minced Garlic
- 2 tbsp. Apple Cider Vinegar
- 2 tbsp. Fresh Lime Juice
- 2 tbsp. Dukes Mayo
- 3 tbsp. Aji Panca Paste
- 1/2 cup Soy Sauce
- 1/2 cup Guinness Extra Stout Dark Beer
- 1 cup Olive Oil

SEASONINGS:
- 4 tsp. Salt
- 4 tsp. Black Pepper
- 2 tsp. Oregano
- 2 tsp. Cumin

DIRECTIONS:
1. Preheat oven to 400 degrees.
2. Start by removing the insides from the Chicken. Then rinse the Chicken in cool water and Lemon Juice. Remove from the water bath and pat dry.
3. To make the cooking process shorter, you want to spatch-cock the Chicken. Take a pair of shears and remove the backbone from the Chicken by cutting along the spine down to the tail.
4. Once the backbone has been removed, take a small knife and poke several holes throughout the Chicken. (Creating little pockets for the marinade) Place the Chicken into a deep baking dish and set aside to prepare the marinade.
5. Now, let's prepare the star of our dish- the marinade. In a medium mixing bowl, combine a half cup of Olive Oil, Apple Cider Vinegar, Soy Sauce, Guinness Extra Stout Dark Beer, minced Garlic, fresh Rosemary, Oregano, Cumin, a couple of teaspoons of Salt along with Black pepper, and finally two tablespoons of Aji Panca Paste. This flavorful blend will infuse the

Chicken with a delicious taste. Pour the marinade over the Chicken, then be sure that the marinade gets all over the Chicken. Place the baking dish into the fridge for an hour to allow the marinade to seep through the Chicken.

6. Once the hour has passed, take the baking dish from the fridge and place the Chicken onto a wire rack. (DO NOT THROW AWAY THE MARINADE)

7. Now, it's time to let the oven work its magic. Place the Chicken into the oven UNCOVERED for 1 hour. Don't worry about the Chicken drying out- we'll be basting it with the leftover marinade every 20 minutes. This step is crucial to keep the Chicken moist and flavorful. Once complete, remove the Chicken from the oven and set aside to prepare the sauce. Into a food processor, add in Cilantro, Green Onions, Jalapeno, Garlic Cloves, Fresh Lime Juice, three tablespoons of Olive Oil, Mayo of choice, a tablespoon of Aji Panca Paste, and a couple of teaspoons of Salt and Black Pepper, then blend.

8. Break down the Chicken once the sauce is ready by cutting each piece and enjoying it with your favorite sides! ENJOY!

FULLY LOADED BAKED POTATO

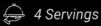 4 Servings Recipe 1 Hour 15 Minutes

INGREDIENTS:
- (1) lb. Large Raw Shrimp
- (4) Russet Potatoes
- (2) Ribeye Steaks
- (1) Broccoli Head
- 2 tbsp. Butter, salted
- 2 tbsp. Minced Garlic
- 2 tbsp. Minced Shallots
- 4 tbsp. Fresh Parsley
- 1 cup Olive Oil
- 1 cup Heavy Cream
- 1 cup Parmesan Cheese, shredded

SEASONINGS:
- 4 tsp Nick's Zesty Steak Seasoning
- 2 tsp Nick's Brandied Pepper Seasoning
- 2 tsp Kinder's Cracked Pepper & Lemon Seasoning
- 2 tsp Smoked Paprika
- 2 tsp. Tabitha Brown's Very Good Garlic Seasoning
- 2 tsp. Southern-Made Creole Seasoning

DIRECTIONS:
1. Preheat the oven/air fryer to 400 degrees.
2. Rinse the potatoes under cool water and gently brush off any remaining dirt. A vegetable brush can make this task even more accessible.
3. Once complete, pat the potatoes dry, then grab a fork or knife, whichever is easiest. Poke holes through the entire potato. This allows the steam to escape during cooking, ensuring the potato cooks thoroughly once in the oven or air fryer.
4. Lay the potatoes on a baking sheet. Pour a couple tablespoons of olive oil on each potato, then rub it in to coat it well. Next, season the potatoes on all sides with Nick's branded pepper, then place the baking sheet in the oven or air fryer.
5. Cook the potatoes for 45-55 minutes, ensuring to flip them halfway through the cooking process. This step is crucial for even cooking. Once they are complete, remove the potatoes from the oven/air fryer, then set aside to prepare Broccoli, Steak, and Shrimp.

6. Rinse, peel, and devein the shrimp, then cut the Steak into 2-inch cubes. Break down the Broccoli into florets to make it easier to cook. Next, add the steak, shrimp, and broccoli to separate bowls for seasonings. Pour a couple of tablespoons of Olive oil on the Shrimp and Broccoli first, then season the steak with Nick's Zesty Steak seasoning.

7. Season the Broccoli with Nick's branded pepper, and mix the Shrimp with Kinder's Cracked Pepper & Lemon seasoning, Smoked Paprika, and fresh Parsley. In a medium skillet on high heat, pour in a couple of tablespoons of Olive Oil, then add the seasoned steak bites. Sear the steak on each side for a minute, then remove them from the skillet and into a bowl.

8. In the same skillet, reduce the heat to medium, then add the shrimp. Sear them on each side for 3-5 minutes. Then, once they are done, remove them from the skillet and put them into a separate bowl from the steak.

9. Finally, spread the broccoli on a baking tray. Place the tray in the oven or air fryer and cook the broccoli for 12-14 minutes at 375 degrees, shaking it halfway through.

10. After cooking, remove the potatoes from the oven or air fryer. Then, it's time to make the sauce. Reduce the heat in the skillet to medium/low, then melt a couple of tablespoons of Butter. Once melted, toss in some minced Garlic and Shallots.

11. Saute the shallots and garlic for a few minutes, then pour in the Heavy Cream. Season the sauce with Tabitha Brown's Very Good Garlic seasoning and Southern Made Creole seasoning. Next, add a little shredded Parmesan cheese and Parsley. Mix.

12. Bring the sauce to a simmer, and once it has reached a satisfactory consistency, cut the heat and assemble the Potatoes. Cut the potatoes down the middle with a knife, then add some sauce, then broccoli, more sauce, the steak, more sauce, shrimp, and of course, more sauce! Sprinkle on a little more Parmesan Cheese and Parsley.

13. Nothing left to do is dig in! ENJOY!

JAMAICAN CURRY CHICKEN

 4 Servings   *Recipe*   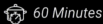 *60 Minutes*

INGREDIENTS:
- (4) Leg Quarters
- (4) Thyme Spriggs
- (4) Yukon Gold Potatoes, Rough Cut
- (3) Carrot Stalks, Rough Cut
- (2) Green Onion Stalks, Chopped
- (1) can Native Forest Organic Unsweetened Coconut Cream
- (1) Green Pepper, Sliced
- (1) Yellow Pepper, Sliced
- (1) Red Pepper, Sliced
- (1) Scotch Bonnet, Habanero Pepper
- 3 tbsp. Minced Garlic
- 3 tbsp. Minced Ginger
- 2 tsp Water
- 1 tsp Cornstarch
- 1/2 cup Hot Water
- 1 cup Olive Oil

SEASONINGS:
- 1/4 cup Whole Allspice
- 4 tbsp. Betapac Curry Powder
- 2 tbsp. Chicken Seasoning
- 2 tbsp. Spice Theory Jerk Spice Rub
- 1 tbsp. Osmo Chicken & Herbs Sea Salt

DIRECTIONS:
1. Remove the leg quarters from the package, rinse the Chicken in cool water and Lemon Juice, and then pat dry.
2. Cut the leg quarters into three-inch pieces by taking a large chef's knife and chopping the Chicken down to shorten the cooking process.
3. Once the Chicken has been chopped down, add the piece to a mixing bowl for seasoning. Pour in three tablespoons of Olive Oil, then season with Chicken seasoning and two tablespoons of Betapac Curry Powder seasoning. Toss in a few fresh Thyme Spriggs and chopped Green Onions, then mix.
4. In a large pot on medium heat, pour in three tablespoons of Olive Oil. Once the oil is ready, add sliced onions, minced Garlic, a couple of sprigs of Thyme, and two tablespoons of Betapac Curry Powder.
5. Saute the veggies and spice for a few minutes, then add the Chicken. Sear the Chicken on each side for 5-7 minutes, then pour in a can of Coconut

Cream and hot water. Season the pot with whole Allspice, Spice Theory Jerk Spice Rub, and Osmo Chicken & Herbs sea salt, then mix.

6. Place a lid on and slow boil for 20 minutes. Once the time is up, remove the lid, stir the Chicken, and add the final veggies to the pot: ginger, sliced green, yellow, and red peppers, a scotch bonnet, potatoes, and carrots.

7. Pour in a cornstarch slurry by combining cornstarch and water; this can help thicken the sauce as it cooks. Give everything one final mix, then place the lid back on and cook for 25 minutes on medium heat.

8. Once the 25 minutes have passed, cut the heat, take the lid off and give your delicious Jamaican Curry Chicken a stir. The rich aroma and vibrant colors of the dish will surely whet your appetite. Grab a couple bowls for you and the family, fill it with white rice with this amazing curry on top and savor the satisfaction of a job well done. ENJOY!

JAMAICAN JERK CHICKEN

 4 Servings   Recipe   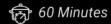 60 Minutes

INGREDIENTS:
- (4) Leg Quarters
- (3) Thyme Sprigs
- (3) Garlic Cloves
- (3) Nutmeg Cloves
- (3) Cinnamon Sticks
- (3) Green Onion Stalks, Chopped
- (2) Scotch Bonnet, Habanero Pepper
- (1) Red Onion, Chopped
- (1) Orange, Freshly Squeezed
- (1) Lime, Freshly Squeezed
- (1) Red Stripe, Bottle
- 3 tbsp. Ginger, Chopped
- 3 tbsp. Soy Sauce
- 3 tbsp. Browning
- 3 tbsp. Vinegar
- 1 tbsp. Walkerwood Green Seasoning
- 1 cup Olive Oil

SEASONINGS:
- 1/4 cup Whole Allspice
- 4 tsp. Granulated Chicken Bouillon Seasoning

DIRECTIONS:
1. Heat a skillet on medium heat. Add whole Nutmeg, a few Cinnamon Sticks, and a couple tablespoons of Allspice. Toast the spices for 5-7 minutes or until you begin to smell the spices wafting from the skillet.
2. After the spices are ground, take a moment to relax. Turn off the skillet, add the spices to a spice grinder, and set them aside for a few minutes.
3. To a food processor, add in Green Onions, a few Thyme sprigs, chopped Ginger, diced Red Onions, a couple of Garlic cloves, a few Scotch Bonnets, about three tablespoons of Olive Oil, freshly squeezed Orange, and Lime juice, Soy Sauce, Browning, and finally the spice mix we just created. Blend.
4. Remove the leg quarters from the package, rinse the chicken in cool water, add vinegar and lime juice, and then pat them dry.
5. Cut slits into the leg quarters, then season the chicken with Granulated Chicken Bouillon seasoning, Walkerwood's Green seasoning, and that

homemade Jerk season we made earlier, then massage into the leg quarters making sure to get in between the slits of the chicken as well.

6. Next, start the grill, and once it is ready, add the Leg Quarters skin side down. Sear each Leg Quarter over the open flames for 8-10 minutes or until they have a nice char on them, then move them to the cool side of the grill. Close the top on the grill to allow the chicken to bake for 15-20 minutes.

7. Open the grill's top, pop open a Red Stripe, and marinate the leg quarters by sprinkling the beer and brushing on the jerk marinade the chicken was in. This will keep the chicken nice and juicy while it bakes on the grill. Close the top and allow the chicken to cook for 20-25 minutes or until they reach an internal temperature of 165 degrees.

8. Once done, remove them from the grill and onto a cutting board. Cut the leg quarters into three-inch pieces by taking a large chef's knife and chopping the Chicken down.

9. Finally, grab a bowl filled with Rice and Peas and that delicious Jerk Chicken, and ENJOY!

GARLIC PARMESAN LAMB CHOPS

 4 Servings Recipe 20 Minutes

INGREDIENTS:
- 2 lbs Lamb Chops
- (1) Lemon, Freshly Squeezed
- Fresh Parsley
- 4 tbsp Olive Oil
- 4 tbsp Butter, Salted
- 4 tbsp Worcestershire Sauce

SEASONINGS:
- 2 tsp Spiceology Cajun Seasoning
- 2 tsp Black Garlic Seasoning
- 2 tsp Italian Herb Seasoning

DIRECTIONS:
1. Remove your Lamb from its package and pat dry as much moisture as possible to ensure seasonings stick, then place them in a large mixing bowl.
2. Pour in Worcestershire Sauce then season the chops with Spiceology Cajun seasoning, Black Garlic, and Italian Herb seasoning. Massage ingredients into the Lamb Chops on both sides then set aside to prepare the skillet.
3. Into a 12-inch skillet on medium/high heat, pour in Olive Oil then the Lamb Chops. Depending on the size of the Lamb Chops, you want to sear for 2-4 minutes on each side.
4. Once the Lamb Chops are done to your desired temperature, remove them from the skillet and set them aside to prepare Garlic Parmesan Butter Sauce.
5. In a small saucepan on low heat, melt half a stick of salted Butter. Once melted, add in freshly minced Garlic, freshly squeezed Lemon Juice and Parsley.

6. Allow the sauce to come to a simmer then reduce shut off the heat and sprinkle in a little parmesan cheese then mix and set aside.
7. Finally, plate Lamb Chops on top of a bed of Garlic Mash Potatoes, drizzle on that Garlic Parmesan Butter Sauce, sprinkle a little more Parmesan Cheese on top and ENJOY!

SIDE DISHES

OVEN BAKED BEANS

 5 Servings   Recipe   1 Hour 20 Minutes

INGREDIENTS:
- 10 oz Pack of Godshall's Beef Bacon
- 1 lb Ground Beef
- 1 lb Bush's Beans Original
- 1 lb Bush's Beans Honey Sweet
- 1/3 cup White Onions, Diced
- 1/3 cup Green Bell Peppers, Diced
- 1/3 cup Red Bell Peppers, Diced
- 1/4 cup Mustard
- 1/8 cup Worcestershire Sauce
- 1/2 cup Brown Sugar
- 1 cup Nick's Barbecue Sauce

SEASONINGS:
- 2 tbsp Nick's Branded Pepper Seasoning
- 2 tbsp Spice King Country BBQ Rub

DIRECTIONS:
1. Preheat oven to 350 degrees.
2. Remove bacon from its package, grab a cutting board, and dice bacon. In a medium skillet on medium/high heat, add diced Beef Bacon.
3. Cook bacon for 10 minutes or until crispy, then remove from the skillet and place bacon bits in a bowl lined with paper towels to help drain the grease from the bacon.
4. In a large skillet on medium/high heat, add Ground Beef to one side of the pan, and on the other side, add diced Onions, Green Bell Pepper, and Red Bell Pepper.
5. Break down ground beef with a meat masher, mix in veggies with the beef, then season with Nick's Branded Pepper Seasoning and Spice King Country BBQ Rub, then mix.
6. Cook your meat mixture for 8-10 minutes or until it gets brown, then turn off the heat and sit aside.
7. In a large baking dish, pour in 1 can of Bush's Beans Original and one can of Bush's Beans Honey Sweet, then mix.

8. Next, add in Ground Beef mixture, diced Beef Bacon, Nick's Barbecue Sauce, Mustard, Worcestershire Sauce, and finally Brown Sugar, then mix until ingredients are well incorporated.
9. Cover the baking dish with foil, then place the dish in preheated oven to cook for an hour.
10. Once complete, remove from the oven, grab a bowl, fill it with your Baked Beans, and ENJOY!

SAUTÉED GREEN BEANS

 3 Servings   Recipe   15 Minutes

INGREDIENTS:
- 1 lb Fresh Green Beans
- Half White Onion, Sliced
- 2 tbsp Avocado Oil
- 4 tbsp Kerry Gold Garlic & Herb Butter
- 1/4 cup Chicken Broth

SEASONINGS:
- 2 tbsp Garlic & Herb Seasoning
- 1 tbsp All-Purpose Seasoning

DIRECTIONS:
1. Start by slicing your White Onion, then rinse Green Beans in cool water.
2. Once you have sliced the onions, place them in a small ramekin, place the Green Beans in a mixing bowl, and then set aside a bit.
3. In a skillet on medium/high heat, melt 2 tbsp of Butter, and once melted, add in sliced White Onions along with the Green Beans.
4. Sauté the Green Beans and Onions for 3-4 minutes, then add another 2 tbsp of Butter and a little Avocado Oil.
5. Sauté them for 2-3 minutes before adding Chicken Broth. Allow the Chicken Broth to soak into the Green Beans for a bit.
6. You will know they are finished once you notice that most broth has evaporated from the pan.
7. Turn off the heat, give your Green Beans another good stir, and serve these on the side with any recipe and ENJOY!

SEAFOOD PASTA SALAD

 4 Servings   Recipe   30 Minutes

INGREDIENTS:
- 1 lb Jumbo Shrimp
- 1 lb Jumbo Lump Crab Meat
- 7 oz Lobster Meat, fully cooked
- 12oz Box Rotini Noodles
- 1/2 Red Onion, Diced
- 1 Red Bell Pepper, Diced
- 1 Green Bell Pepper, Diced
- 1/4 cup Green Onions, Sliced
- 1/4 cup Sweet Relish
- 1/3 cup Mustard
- 1/2 cup Avocado Oil
- 1 cup Mayo
- 4 tbsp Butter, Salted

SEASONINGS:
- 1/3 cup King Crab ATL Seafood Seasoning
- 1/3 cup McCormick Salad Supreme
- 2 tbsp White Salt
- 2 tsp Black Pepper
- 1 tsp Smoked Paprika

DIRECTIONS:
1. Rinse off the shrimp under cool water, then peel the shrimp, removing the tail as well. Once peeled, pat dry, then place shrimp into a mixing bowl.
2. Next, pour 2 tbsp of Avocado Oil into the mixing bowl and 2 tsp of King Crab ATL Seafood Seasoning and Smoked Paprika, then mix until well combined.
3. In a medium skillet on medium/high heat, pour in 2 tbsp of Avocado Oil along with your shrimp that was just seasoned.
4. Cook the shrimp for 3-4 minutes on one side, then flip, toss in 2 tbsp of butter, and cook shrimp for two more minutes while stirring in the butter.
5. After the shrimp have finished cooking, remove them from the skillet, sit them aside, and add another 2 tbsp of butter along with the Lobster meat. You don't need to cook Lobster meat long because it is fully cooked. Only cook for 2-3 minutes to allow butter into the Lobster meat. Could you remove them from the skillet when finished and sit aside? (If you have fresh Lobster, do the same process as Step 4)

6. In a medium pot, start boiling 3 cups of water with salt. Once the water begins to boil, add the pasta and cook for 9min, stirring occasionally. Once finished, drain off the water, run the pasta under cool water to stop it from further cooking, and place the pasta into a large mixing bowl. Add the Shrimp, Lobster, and Jumbo Lump Crab meat in that same bowl and all of your diced vegetables, followed by Mayo, Mustard, and Sweet Relish, then mix until well combined.

7. Season the Seafood Pasta Salad with the rest of the King Crab ATL Seafood Seasoning, McCormick Salad Supreme, and Black Pepper, then mix a final time, and it is complete.

8. Fill a few bowls with your Seafood Pasta Salad with a side of your favorite crackers, and ENJOY!

SALMON CAESAR PASTA SALAD

 4 Servings   Recipe   35 Minutes

INGREDIENTS:
- 1 lb Atlantic Salmon
- (1) Romaine Lettuce Head
- (1) Red Onion, Sliced
- (3) Carrots, Shredded
- (4) Cento Flat Fillet Anchovies (FOR DRESSING)
- (6) Garlic Cloves (FOR DRESSING)
- 2 tbsp Worcestershire Sauce (FOR DRESSING)
- 2 tbsp Grey Poupon Dijon Mustard (FOR DRESSING)
- 4 tbsp Extra Virgin Olive Oil (FOR SALMON)
- 2/3 cup Extra Virgin Olive Oil (FOR DRESSING)
- 1 cup Mayo of choice (FOR DRESSING)
- 1/4 cup Grated Parmesan Cheese

SEASONINGS:
- 2 tbsp Spice King Gourmet Seafood Seasoning
- 1 tsp Salt
- 1 tsp Fresh Cracked Black Pepper

DIRECTIONS:
1. Preheat oven to 350 degrees.
2. Remove the Salmon from the package and lay the Salmon on a parchment paper-lined baking sheet for seasonings.
3. Next, pour Extra Virgin Olive Oil over the Salmon, then season with Garlic Herb, Lemon Pepper Seasoning, Jerk Seasoning, and Smoked Paprika.
4. Massage in the seasonings on both sides, then place the Salmon into the oven and cook for 15-20 minutes or until the Salmon reaches an internal temp of 145 degrees.
5. Once complete, remove the Salmon from the oven, break it into smaller pieces, add the salmon to a medium mixing bowl, and then set it aside.
6. Bring 4-6 quarts of water to a boil in a medium pot on high heat. Once the water is boiling, turn the heat to medium, then heavily salt the water and add in a box of Rotini pasta.

7. Cook the pasta for 8-10 minutes, then shut off the heat, drain the water from the pasta, add the pasta to the mixing bowl with the Salmon in it, and set the bowl aside.
8. Chop the stalk from Romaine Lettuce head. Afterward, cool water over the lettuce head to clean it and keep it from softening.
9. After rinsing them off, chop about 3 cups worth of lettuce, then add it to the bowl with the pasta and salmon, then set the bowl aside to prepare Homemade Caesar Dressing.

HOMEMADE CAESAR DRESSING

1. Into a blender, add Garlic Cloves, Flat Fillet Anchovies, Worcestershire Sauce, Grey Poupon Dijon Mustard, Mayo of choice, 2/3 cups of Extra Virgin Olive Oil, 1/4 cups of Grated Parmesan Cheese, Salt, and Fresh Cracked Black Pepper.
2. Blend for 2-3 minutes to ensure the ingredients mix well, then build your Salmon Caesar Salad and ENJOY.

SOUTHERN STYLE COLLARD GREENS

 4 Servings   *Recipe*   *1 Hour 40 Minutes*

INGREDIENTS:
- (1) Pack Smoked Turkey Necks
- (1) Yellow Onion, Sliced
- (1) Red Bell Pepper, Sliced
- 3 lbs of Collard Greens
- 1/4 cup Brown Sugar
- 4 cup Chicken Broth
- 3 tbsp Avocado Oil
- 2 tbsp Minced Garlic
- 1 tsp Better Than Bouillon Roasted Chicken Base

SEASONINGS:
- 2 tsp Simply Spicy Spice All-Purpose Seasoning
- 2 tsp Simply Spicy Spice Garlic Herb Lemon Pepper Seasoning
- 2 tsp Smoked Paprika
- 2 tsp Black Pepper
- 2 tsp Crushed Red Pepper Flakes

DIRECTIONS:
1. Begin by rinsing the Greens in cool water. Afterward, remove the stems by carefully cutting alongside the leaf where it meets the stem on both sides.
2. Once you have removed the stems from all the Greens, roll them like you are rolling a burrito and break down the collards by cutting 1-inch rolls out.
3. Cut down the middle of the rolls, then place the Greens in a large mix bowl with a generous amount of Himalayan Sea Salt and cool water.
4. Clean the Greens thoroughly until the water runs clear. Once complete, set them aside.
5. In a large boiling pot on medium/high heat, pour in a little Avocado oil and the sliced Yellow Onion, Red Bell Pepper, Minced Garlic, and Badia Complete Seasoning.
6. Sauté the veggies for 5-7 minutes, add the Smoked Turkey neck and Chicken Broth, then mix everything well. Place a lid on the pot and bring it to a boil.

7. Once boiling, add in the Greens. Depending on how much you have, gradually add the Greens into the pot one handful at a time until all of them are in there.
8. Next, season the Greens with Simply Spicy Spice All-Purpose Seasoning, Simply Spicy Spice Garlic Herb Lemon Pepper Seasoning, Smoked Paprika, Black Pepper, Crushed Red Pepper Flakes, Brown Sugar, and Better Than Bouillon Roasted Chicken Base then mix.
9. Place the lid back on and cook the Greens for 1 hour and 30 minutes. Once time has passed, the Turkey neck should be nice and tender, and removing the meat from the bone should be easy.
10. Remove the meat from the Turkey Neck bones, place the turkey meat back in with the greens, then stir until well combined. Also, you can either toss the bones out or put them back in the Greens for that extra flavor!
11. Grab yourself a bowl of those delicious Collard Greens with a piece of Honey Cornbread on the side, and ENJOY!

CAJUN STYLE FRIED CABBAGE

 5 Servings   Recipe   35 Minutes

INGREDIENTS:
- (1) Cabbage Head
- (1) Yellow Onion, Chopped
- (1) Red Bell Pepper, Chopped
- (1) Green Bell Pepper, Chopped
- (1) Pack Godshall's Beef Bacon
- (1) Pack Hillshire Farm Cajun Style Andouille Smoked Sausage
- 3 tbsp Olive Oil

SEASONINGS:
- 3 tbsp Badia Complete Seasoning
- 3 tbsp Tabitha Brown's Very Good Garlic Seasoning
- 3 tbsp Spiceology Cajun Seasoning
- 3 tbsp Southern Made Creole Seasoning

DIRECTIONS:
1. Begin by removing the two outer layers of the Cabbage, then rinse the Cabbage under cold water. Pat the cabbage dry, then cut the core off.
2. Next, cut the cabbage in half and remove the rest of the core. Once the core has been removed, cut the cabbage down into cubes or slices, depending on preference.
3. Place Cabbage in a strainer and rinse Cabbage off for a final time; drain the water, then place into a bowl and set aside for later.
4. Next, do a rough cut of the Onions and Red and Green Peppers, place them in another bowl, and set aside to prepare the bacon and sausage.
5. Dice a pack of GodShall's Beef Bacon maple bacon, then take a package of Hillshire Farm Cajun Style Andouille Smoked Sausage and slice it into half-inch pieces. Place these two proteins into two bowls, then move to the next step.
6. In a large boiling pot on medium/high heat, pour in a couple tablespoons of Olive Oil. First, add in the sausage. Cook the sausage for 4 minutes on

each side to get a nice char on them. Once done, remove them from the pot and put them into a bowl lined with napkins.

7. Afterwards, add the bacon to the same pot, then cook it for 5-7 minutes or just until it has a nice crisp. Once done, remove the bacon from the pot, put it into a bowl lined with napkins, and set aside.

8. In the same pot, add minced garlic and sauté for a few minutes so that the garlic can incorporate itself with the flavors left behind from the bacon and sausage.

9. Once the garlic has sautéed, toss in the Onions, Red and Green Peppers, and Badia Complete seasoning. Then, just like the garlic, you want to sauté them for a few minutes to seal in all that flavor for the cabbage.

10. Finally, add the cabbage and season it with Tabitha Brown's Very Good Garlic seasoning, Spiceology Cajun seasoning, and Southern Made Creole seasoning, then give everything a good mix together. Reduce the heat to low and cover the pot with a lid. Because Cabbage already retains water, there is no need to add any extra water or broth into the mix. It will produce enough for the cabbage to cook in its juices.

11. Allow the cabbage to cook for 10-15 minutes while stirring periodically. Depending on how you enjoy the texture of your Cabbage, you can choose to stop cooking it at the end of the 10-15 minutes or continue cooking for an additional 5 minutes.

12. Kill the heat, grab a couple of bowls, add some of that delicious Cabbage, and serve it with hot Honey Cornbread! Enjoy!

DESSERTS

PEACH COBBLER EGG ROLLS

 3 Servings   *Recipe*   *30 Minutes*

INGREDIENTS:

- (8) Egg Roll Wrappers
- (2) Scoops of Vanilla Bean Ice Cream (OPTIONAL)
- 1 cup Sliced Peaches
- 2 cups Vegetable Cooking Oil
- 1/2 cup Brown Sugar
- 1/2 cup White Sugar
- 1/2 cup McCormick Cinnamon Sugar
- 1/4 cup Water
- 4 tbsp Caramel (OPTIONAL)
- 4 tbsp Unsalted Sweet Butter
- 3 tbsp Fresh Lemon Juice
- 2 tbsp Pure Vanilla Extract
- 2 tbsp Nutmeg
- 2 tbsp Cinnamon
- 2 Shots of Crown Royal Peach
- 1 tsp Cornstarch

DIRECTIONS:

1. Begin by melting half a stick of butter in a medium skillet on low heat. Once the butter has melted, add the sliced peaches and a bit of the juice they were sitting in.
2. Next, add in Brown Sugar, White Sugar, Cinnamon, Nutmeg, Pure Vanilla Extract, a couple shots of Crown Royal Peach, fresh Lemon Juice, and a cornstarch slurry made with a bit of cornstarch mixed with water.
3. Give everything a good mix together, then crank the heat up to medium and let your Peach mixture get a little thick and come to a simmer.
4. Allow your peaches to simmer for 3-5 minutes before removing them from the heat and setting them aside to begin rolling them in Egg Rolls.
5. Grab about 8 Egg Roll Wrappers or as many as you need to stuff all the Peaches into them, then make another Cornstarch slurry. This will help seal the egg rolls after you roll them.

6. Lay out one of the Egg Roll Wrappers in a diamond shape before you, then add some slurry to the corners of the egg roll.
7. Add the Peach filling to the middle, then take the closest corner to you and fold over the peach filling. Next, fold in the right side, then the left, and roll until closed. Then repeat for the rest of the egg rolls.
8. Seal the egg rolls off with a little more slurry, making sure there are no openings, then set them aside to prepare the cooking oil.
9. In a 5-quart pot, pour 2 cups of Vegetable Cooking Oil, then turn the heat to medium. Allow the cooking oil to reach a temperature of 350 degrees, then begin adding the egg rolls.
10. Allow the Egg Rolls to cook for 3-5 minutes or until golden brown, then remove them from the oil and place them on a wire rack to drain any extra oil off.
11. While the Egg Rolls are still nice and hot, add some McCormick Cinnamon Sugar to a bowl and roll them around, giving them a sweet coating on the outside of the egg rolls.
12. Finally, add some Egg Rolls to a bowl with some Vanilla Bean Ice Cream with a drizzle of Caramel, and ENJOY!

APPLE PIE EGG ROLLS

INGREDIENTS:
- (8-10) Egg Roll Wrappers
- (4) Fresh Red Apples, peeled & cubed
- (2) Scoops of Vanilla Bean Ice Cream (OPTIONAL)
- (2) Shots of Crown Royal Apple (OPTIONAL)
- 3 tbsp. Unsalted Sweet Butter
- 3 tbsp. Fresh Lemon Juice
- 3 tbsp. Brown Sugar
- 2 tbsp. White Sugar
- 2 tsp. Pure Vanilla Extract
- 2 tsp. Nutmeg
- 2 tsp. Cinnamon
- 1 tsp. Cornstarch
- 1/4 cup Water
- 3-4 cups Vegetable Cooking Oil

DIRECTIONS:
1. Begin by peeling and cutting the apples into cubes.
2. Melt two tablespoons of butter in a medium skillet on medium heat. Once the butter has melted, add the Apples to the skillet.
3. Next, add Brown Sugar, White Sugar, Cinnamon, Nutmeg, Pure Vanilla Extract, a couple of shots of Crown Royal Apple, and freshly squeezed Lemon Juice.
4. Give everything a good mix, then increase the heat a bit to reduce the liquor and allow the sauce to thicken up.
5. Allow the apple filling to simmer for 6-8 minutes before removing it from the heat and putting it in a mixing bowl. Set it aside to begin rolling it in egg rolls.
6. Grab 8-10 Egg Roll Wrappers or as many as you need to stuff all the Peaches into them, then make another Cornstarch slurry. This will help seal the egg rolls after you roll them.

7. Lay out one of the Egg Roll Wrappers in a diamond shape before you, then add some slurry to the corners of the egg roll.
8. Add the Apple filling to the middle, then take the closest corner to you and fold over the Apple filling. Next, fold in the right side, then the left, and roll until closed. Then repeat for the rest of the egg rolls.
9. Seal the egg rolls off with a little more slurry, making sure there are no openings, then set them aside to prepare the cooking oil.
10. In a 5-quart pot, pour in Vegetable Cooking Oil, then turn the heat medium. Allow the cooking oil to reach a temperature of 350-365 degrees, then begin adding in the egg rolls.
11. Allow the Egg Rolls to cook for 3-5 minutes or until golden brown, then remove them from the oil and onto a wire rack to drain any extra oil off.
12. While the Egg Rolls are still nice and hot, sprinkle on a little Cinnamon Toast Crunch Cinnadust, giving them a sweet coating on the outside of the egg rolls.
13. Finally, add some Apple Pie Egg Rolls to a bowl with some Vanilla Bean Ice Cream, and ENJOY!

FRIED APPLE DUMP CAKE

 3 Servings   **Recipe**   **1 Hour**

INGREDIENTS:
- (2) Scoops of Caramel Swirl Ice Cream (OPTIONAL)
- (3) Fresh Apples, peeled & sliced
- 1 cup AP Flour
- 1.5 cup White Sugar
- 1/2 cup Brown Sugar
- 1/4 cup Water
- 8 tbsp Salted Sweet Butter
- 4 tbsp Unsalted Sweet Butter
- 3 tbsp Fresh Lemon Juice
- 2 tbsp Pure Vanilla Extract
- 2 tbsp Nutmeg
- 2 tbsp Cinnamon
- 2 Shots of Crown Royal Apple
- 1 tsp Cornstarch
- 1 tsp Baking Powder
- 1 tsp Baking Soda
- 1 tsp Salt

DIRECTIONS:
1. Preheat oven to 350 degrees, then begin peeling and cutting the apples into slices.
2. Melt half a stick of butter in a medium skillet on low heat. Once the butter has melted, add the sliced Apples.
3. Next, add in Brown Sugar, White Sugar, Cinnamon, Nutmeg, Pure Vanilla Extract, a couple shots of Crown Royal Apple, fresh Lemon Juice, and a cornstarch slurry made with a bit of cornstarch mixed with water.
4. Give everything a good mix together, then increase the heat to medium to let the Apple filling get thick and come to a simmer.
5. Allow the Apple filling to simmer for 3-5 minutes before removing them from the heat and add the filling to an oven-safe baking dish. Then, set them aside to prepare the Homemade Cake Mix.
6. In a medium mixing bowl, combine the following ingredients: AP Flour, a cup of White Sugar, a teaspoon of Baking Powder, Baking Soda, and Salt, then mix until well combined.

7. Spread your Homemade Cake Mix over the top of the Apple filling, ensuring it is spread evenly throughout the top.
8. Next, cut a whole stick of SALTED Butter into half-inch individual squares, then place them evenly on top of the cake mix.
9. Sprinkle on a little more Cinnamon then place the baking dish in the oven for 45 minutes or until the top of the Dump Cake is golden brown.
10. Once you see that beautiful golden crust on top, remove the dish from the oven and allow it to cool for 5 minutes.
11. Grab a couple of bowls with a couple of scoops of this delicious Fried Apple Dump Cake and enjoy with some ice cream on the side!

SWEET POTATO COBBLER

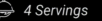 *4 Servings*   *Recipe*   *50 Minutes*

INGREDIENTS:
- (3) Sweet Potatoes, Peeled & Sliced
- (1) Stick of Unsalted Sweet Butter
- (1) Egg
- (1) Pepperidge Farm Puff Pastry Sheet
- 1/4 cup White Sugar
- 1/4 cup Brown Sugar
- 1/4 cup Pineapple Mango Juice
- 2 tbsp Pure Vanilla Extract
- 2 tbsp Nutmeg
- 2 tbsp Cinnamon
- 2 Shots of Hennessy

DIRECTIONS:
1. Preheat oven to 350 degrees, then begin peeling and cutting the Sweet Potatoes into coin-shaped slices.
2. Melt a stick of butter in a medium cast iron skillet on low heat. Once the butter has melted, add Brown Sugar, White Sugar, Cinnamon, Nutmeg, Pure Vanilla Extract, a couple of shots of Hennessy, and Pineapple Mango Juice.
3. Give everything a good mix together, then add the Sweet Potato slices. Increase the heat a little, bringing the potatoes to a simmer, then cover with a lid to cook for 15-20 minutes.
4. After the time has passed, turn off the heat and remove the Sweet Potatoes from the skillet along with a little of the sauce. Be sure to leave some sauce behind in the skillet.
5. Remove a sheet of Puff Pastry from the pack and unfold it. Grab a pizza cutter if you have one, and cut out 3-inch rectangles. Before moving the cut piece, crack one egg and brush it on the pastry pieces.

6. Once all the pieces of the pastry are brushed with egg, set aside for the next step. Grab the cast iron skillet in which we prepared the Sweet Potatoes and turn the heat on to medium, bringing the sauce to a slight simmer.

7. Next, add ten pastry pieces to the skillet and cook them for 3 minutes to allow them to puff up a bit. This will serve as the bottom layer for your cobbler.

8. Reduce the heat to low, then add the Sweet Potatoes on top of the pastry piece, then lay the remainder of the pieces on top of the Sweet Potatoes. Cover with enough pastry pieces to ensure it looks almost like an Apple Pie.

9. Sprinkle on a little more Cinnamon along with the sauce you put aside earlier from the skillet on top and place the skillet into the oven for 30 minutes or until the top of the pastry pieces is golden brown.

10. Once complete, remove the skillet from the oven, grab a bowl of this delicious Sweet Potato Cobbler with a side of Vanilla Bean ice cream, and ENJOY!

PEANUT BUTTER COOKIES

 4-6 Servings   *Recipe*   *20 Minutes*

INGREDIENTS:

- 1 1/2 cup Peanut Butter
- 1 cup Brown Sugar
- 2 Eggs
- 1 tbsp Pure Vanilla Extract

DIRECTIONS:

1. Preheat oven to 350 degrees.
2. In a medium mixing bowl, add in Peanut Butter of your choice, Brown Sugar or White Sugar, a couple of Eggs, and a little Pure Vanilla Extract.
3. Give your ingredients a mix until well combined. Place your cookie dough in the fridge for at least an hour for ingredients to bind with one another.
4. Once your dough has chilled, lay out a baking sheet and line with parchment paper or aluminum foil.
5. Depending on how big or small you want your cookies, take that amount into your hand and roll into balls then lay then on baking sheet 2in apart from each other for spacing.
6. Place your cookies in preheated oven and cook for 10-12 minutes. Check your cookie with a toothpick to see if cookies have finished by sticking tooth pick in cookies and if it comes out clean then you have a winner!
7. Remove from oven and place on wire rack then cool for 5 minutes. Once cooled, grab a glass of milk and good luck eating just one! ENJOY!!

HOMEMADE SNICKERDOODLE COOKIES

🍽 *3-4 Servings*   ✂ *Recipe*   🍲 *30 Minutes*

INGREDIENTS:

- 2 Sticks Butter (Unsalted)
- 1 cup Brown Sugar
- 1 cup White Sugar
- 2 1/2 cups AP Flour
- 2 tsp Cream Of Tartar
- 2 Eggs
- 4 tbsp Cinnamon
- 1 tbsp Vanilla Extract
- 1 tsp Baking Soda
- 1 tsp Himalayan Pink Salt

DIRECTIONS:

1. Preheat oven to 400 degrees.
2. In a medium skillet on medium heat, add in 2 Sticks of Unsalted butter and allow your butter to melt. Once melted skim foam of the top of the butter with a spoon. You want to make sure you cook butter on low heat and slow while stirring until Butter starts to brown. This process can take about 10-15 minutes.
3. Once butter is brown remove from heat and sit aside to cool. In a large mixing bowl add in Brown Sugar, White Sugar, and 2 tbsp Cinnamon then mix. Stir in your Brown Butter and mix until mixture looks like wet sand. Add in 2 eggs along with Pure Vanilla Extract then mix until well combined.
4. To that same mix bowl, add in AP Flour, Baking Soda, Cream of Tartar, and Himalayan Salt. Instead of mixing in the ingredients this time, you want to FOLD in your mixture until you can no longer see flour. This will now be your cookie dough. Place your Cookie Dough in the fridge for an hour before baking to allow dough to settle.

5. In a small mixing bowl combine 3 tbsp White Surgar and 2 tbsp Cinnamon to create your Cinnamon Sugar mix for cookie dough.
6. Now that dough has chilled, scoop a teaspoon of dough then roll into balls then one at a time, roll them around in your cinnamon sugar mixture. Place them on a non-stick baking sheet 2 inches apart for spacing then flatten out cookies a bit on top.
7. Place in preheated oven for 6-8 minutes. Once complete, check your cookie with a toothpick to see if cookies have finished by sticking tooth pick in cookies and if it comes out clean then you have a winner!
8. Remove your Homemade Snickerdoodle Cookies from the oven and allow them to rest for 5 minutes before grabbing that bowl of French Vanilla Ice Cream, but once it has ENJOY!

INDEX

L

Lamb Mac N'Cheese 112

M

Marry Me Salmon Pasta 64
Marry Me Steak Pasta 66

N

Nanna's Baked Meatloaf 126

O

One-Pan Chicken & Rice 128
One-Pot Lasagna 136
Oven Baked Beans 156
OVEN-ROASTED BBQ JERK
WINGS 14

P

Parmesan Crusted Salmon 138
Peach Cobbler Egg Rolls 170
Peanut Butter Cookies 178
PEPSI STICKY WINGS 16
POPCORN LOBSTER BITES 34
POT ROAST CORNBREAD
SLIDERS 26

R

Red Velvet Chicken Sandwich 78
Roasted Peruvian Chicken 144

S

Salisbury Steak 140

Salmon Alfredo Lasagna Rolls 74
Salmon Alfredo Stuffed Bell
Peppers 88
Salmon Burger 108
SALMON CAESAR LETTUCE
BOATS 32
Salmon Caesar Pasta Salad 162
Sautéed Green Beans 158
Seafood Gumbo 90
Seafood Pasta Salad 160
Seafood Stuffed Pasta Shells 68
Short Rib Mini Tacos 130
Shrimp Stir Fry 86
Slow Cooked BBQ Beef Tip
Sandwiches 110
Southern Style Collard Greens 164
Spaghetti & Meatballs 134
SPICY BBQ MEATBALL
SLIDERS 28
Spicy Shrimp Pasta 62
Spicy Teriyaki Fried Ribs 120
SPINACH CRAB DIP EGG
ROLLS 22
Steak Alfredo 46
Steak Alfredo French Bread Za 48
Steak Fajitas 116
Steak Foil Wraps 96
Sweet Potato Cobbler 176

T

Tarragon Chicken 44

NOTES

Made in the USA
Monee, IL
04 December 2024

5b9ae573-bf4b-4630-ab2a-293849c9e2deR02